The Poetry Review

The Poetry Society, 22 Betterton Street, London WC2H 9BX

The Poetry Review

The Poetry Society, 22 Betterton Street, London WC2H 9BX
Tel: +44 (0)20 7420 9880 • Fax: +44 (0)20 7240 4818
Email: poetryreview@poetrysociety.org.uk
poetrysociety.org.uk/thepoetryreview

Editor: Emily Berry
Production: Michael Sims

ISBN: 978-1-911046-28-8 ISSN: 0032 2156
Cover artwork: Kate Dehler, katedehler.com
Cover quote by Paula Bohince, see p. 17

...

SUBMISSIONS
We welcome submissions. Guidelines available at poetrysociety.org.uk/thepoetryreview

ADVERTISING
To place advertisements, visit poetrysociety.org.uk/thepoetryreview or contact Ben Rogers on +44 (0)20 7420 9880, email: marketing@poetrysociety.org.uk

BOOKSHOP DISTRIBUTION
Central Books, 50 Freshwater Road, London RM8 1RX, UK. Tel: +44 (0)20 8525 8800 or visit centralbooks.com

PBS OFFER TO POETRY SOCIETY MEMBERS
The Poetry Book Society offers Poetry Society Members a special 10% discount (plus postage) on books bought from poetrybooks.co.uk. For details, contact The Poetry Society: +44 (0)20 7420 9880 or membership@poetrysociety.org.uk

SUBSCRIPTIONS & SALES
Individuals UK: £38 / Europe: £48
Rest of the World: £53 (overseas delivery by airmail)
Single issue: £9.50 plus postage. Order online at poetrysociety.org.uk/shop

Subscribe to the digital version of *The Poetry Review* at exacteditions.com/thepoetryreview
The Poetry Review is on sale in leading bookshops. It is also available on audio CD.

The Poetry Review is the magazine of The Poetry Society and was first published in 1912. A subscription to *The Poetry Review* is included as part of membership of The Poetry Society. Views expressed in *The Poetry Review* are not necessarily those of The Poetry Society; those of individual contributors are not necessarily those of the Editor.

Charity Commission No. 303334.

...

THEPOETRYSOCIETY

Supported using public funding by
ARTS COUNCIL ENGLAND

MIX
Paper from responsible sources
FSC® C010693

The Forest Stewardship Council (FSC) promotes environmentally appropriate, socially beneficial, and economically viable management of the world's forests. By buying products with an FSC label you are supporting the growth of responsible forest management worldwide. The Poetry Review *is printed with vegetable-based inks. Surplus inks, plates and printing blankets are recycled.*

CONTENTS

Poems

Jamie McKendrick	Nugget	7
	St Jerome in Self-isolation	
	Close enough	
Geraldine Clarkson	Everything you told me came untrue,	10
	Pastoral Moment	
Tarn MacArthur	The Bone Caves	13
	The Bone Trowel	
	The Lord of the Isles	
Paula Bohince	The Skunk	16
Mary Jean Chan	Calling Home	19
Amlanjyoti Goswami	Bus routes of childhood	20
	Swing Quartet	
Stephanie Sy-Quia	*from* Amnion	23
Angela Cleland	I'm in Costa with the other new mums again	28
	I'm in Costa with the other new mums again	
	I'm in Costa with the other new mums again	
Natalie Crick	Pearls for Little Girls	30
Hannah Regel	The Deer Hunter	31
Will Stone	Opportunists of Genocide	32
	Black Hole	
Dominic Leonard	The Going	34
	Eclogue	
Hagiwara Sakutarō / Jae Kim	Leaping Over the Earth	36
	Fox	
	Tongueless Truth	
	Grave	

The Poetry Society Annual Lecture Series

Face – Face – Face: A Poet Under the Spell of Loss by Valzhyna Mort 38

Poems

Samatar Elmi	The Snails	49
Vona Groarke	Linkage	50
	Quarantine	

Ishion Hutchinson	A Litany in Time of Plague	54
	Les Murray's Bucket Hat	
Mohammad S. Razai	Between the Latin graces	56
	Hazaristan	
Beverley Bie Brahic	Stylebook	58
	Vanity	
	A Dream Catcher	
Marianne Boruch	I Could Redact Most Parts of Me So Memory	61
Kit Buchan	Kind of morning	65
Helen Farish	Encounter	67
	Woman with Red Bra	
	Muse	
Tarik Dobbs	*the true american* wishes to be well-liked at the ford river rouge plant	70
	the true american will enjoy man's best friend	
Gail McConnell	*from* The Sun is Open	72
Richie McCaffery	Sawdust	76
	Sermon	

Interview

Erkut Tokman talks to Alice Notley 78

Essay

Silence, Sound, Ceremony: Jason Allen-Paisant on m nourbeSe philip 86

Reviews

Karen McCarthy Woolf on Rowan Ricardo Phillips and Valzhyna Mort 96
John Greening reviews Christopher Reid and Heidi Williamson 100
Kit Fan on Shane McCrae and J.O. Morgan 105
Chris Moss reviews *Apocalypse: An Anthology* 110
Ben Wilkinson on Glyn Maxwell and Alan Gillis 115
Kathryn Maris reviews Caroline Bergvall and James Womack 119
Bidisha on Martha Sprackland, Romalyn Ante and Will Harris 124
Stephen Wilson on Anthony Burgess's *Collected Poems* 128
Dzifa Benson reviews eight new pamphlets 132

The National Poetry Competition 2020 winners 139

EDITORIAL

Each time I set out to write an editorial, I have the sense that I'm repeating myself. Most likely I am; I haven't looked back lately to see what I wrote before. "I repeat my themes", as Frederick Seidel wrote, possibly the line of poetry that repeats in my head most.

Valzhyna Mort's powerful lecture 'Face – Face – Face: A Poet Under the Spell of Loss', commissioned for the Poetry Society's Annual Lecture Series and published in this issue, traces the workings of repetition across the violent past and present of her homeland Belarus, and through the language of poetry. What is repeated in a poem is something that bears saying again, because we might not have understood it the first time, or because we are afraid we might forget. "[T]he established cycles of repetition are like spells", Mort writes, "and there's no anti-spell to stop them from happening. The more we repeat, the less power we have over the words and the more power the words have over us. Poetic repetition is about the potency of language and the impotence of its speakers. In our care, language is futile and change is impossible."

I'm often reminded of the person quoted in psychoanalyst Stephen Grosz's collection of fictionalised case histories *The Examined Life* (2013), who insisted: "I want to change, but not if it means changing." To be caught in a cycle of repetition is like trying to change without changing. "And yet look at us, why, so sadly, do we stand in front of the grave unable to step away?" asks the speaker in Hagiwara Sakutarō's 'Grave', translated by Jae Kim. A poem itself may be an act of repetition, a return to a psychic fire that has not yet been put out, like Paula Bohince's 'The Skunk', which reflects on a difficult maternal relationship and the quest to extinguish "a fire living underground for half a century": "I went wild, / memorizing her the way others did 'Ozymandias'." 'Ozymandias' is a poem that, among other things, testifies to the endurance of feelings ("those passions [...] / Which yet survive, stamped on these lifeless things"). They repeat their themes, outlasting death and decay.

Jason Allen-Paisant's essay 'Silence, Sound, Ceremony' looks at the work of m nourbeSe philip, whose long poem *Zong!* itself works with repetition to conjure a lament for the lives lost in the infamous *Zong* massacre. He quotes philip's statement in the poem's 'Notanda' that "there is no telling this story; it must be told". To tell a story without telling it is the impossible conundrum of changing without changing, of making the spell of repetition work for us rather than against us. The persistence of poetry is the belief that one day the spell will be broken, as in Geraldine Clarkson's 'Everything you told me came untrue,' an anti-spell for a series of malign prophecies withstood by the speaker: "the old domestic curse, / that I would never write, / that words would fail to join: / the black source like treacle, stuck, // trickles freer with each poem that comes, / Mother." We repeat our themes, because as Tarn MacArthur writes in 'The Lord of the Isles', "This time tomorrow might be different."

Emily Berry

JAMIE McKENDRICK

Nugget

for Michael Hofmann

The magician Márquez had a dread of gold
and wouldn't wear it. But here I am sitting through
Aussie Gold Hunters – that's enjoyed a lockdown
boom, perhaps for the lure of hidden treasure, or because

these stubbly mates have put their lives on hold
to scour a red desert under a cruel sun,
waving a stick that hums then gives a wail of hope
for what – a bug-sized nugget or a rusted can?

Just yards away in the unprospected zone
– if only they'd swerved instead of keeping straight –
lies a buried glory which they'll never find.

They could almost be poets, the way they
trudge cussedly on, quite oblivious
to all the dross and mess they leave behind.

St Jerome in Self-isolation

It may be a hideous rock I've chosen
for my stretch of picturesque seclusion
but it offers shelves and storage space galore.
What looks like a cave is actually a corridor
so I have a choice between two petrified porches,
to one of which I've rigged some primitive thatch.
I have my reading matter and a pet
to protect me from boredom and of course
my *task*: to render reams of holy writ.
Translating anything is bad enough
but try the Word of God, try wading through
pages of genealogy and petty-minded laws,
then heartbreaking songs out of nowhere,
and sudden genius bursting forth
like a scythed chariot drawn by hippogryphs.

Horridus, atrox, the rock may be,
but tourists relish its jagged menace
and geologists pretend to explain it,
casting doubt on the timeline of creation
as set out on the first page of my opus.
The city's visible in the distance, not close
enough to infect the air but not so far
as to deter the odd pilgrim. I'm here to work
not contemplate the landscape, even if
that's what seems to excite the painters
who visit on weekends and have me pose
bespectacled in sackcloth at my threshold,
stylus in one hand, the other ruffling the beast's mane
– damn their rickety easels and their prying eyes.
And damn this Latin that's not Illyrian.

Close enough

for Bernard O'Donoghue

Does earth take a capital letter?
you rightly wonder.
To flatten or flatter
the planet, that seems the question.
And since the matter
concerns a translation
from Dante, a stretch of his hell
where the not-yet-dead
are already embedded
while their neighbours wear owl
heads twisted front-to-back – the horror of error –
it's hard not to hear terra and terror
as almost the same
or a close enough rhyme.

GERALDINE CLARKSON

Everything you told me came untrue,

as if your eye at the witching hour,
when you told us bedtime stories,
was faulty on its target.

Perhaps your seer's hands, smooth
and oiled from washing up, slipped
in their tracing of force-lines
on your crystal ball.

Maybe your too-hasty breath
flustered the tea leaves,
distorted picture portents
dredged on china.

Your prophecy that I might die
young, slipped into disuse
after you'd aired it eighteen times,
once each birthday, for bad luck.

The blade of your sibyl's claim
that I wasn't meant for marriage,
that lovers would recoil,
blunted (though I grasped it still).

And the old domestic curse,
that I would never write,
that words would fail to join:
the black source like treacle, stuck,

trickles freer with each poem that comes,
Mother.

Pastoral Moment
after Mary Jo Bang

A sharp lull on a sheep hill in Dorset:
frontdrop to artless coincidences & airless
confidences from a thrice-divorced roué
from Hull, originally; milkspracht & plausible.
I basket-weave pleasure
on a makeshift loom, schooled
to give as much as I get.
                                        Blue-grey
mist palls the genteel hill, like a lady's
drawstring bonnet: candied evening light,
then a rush of soft-peeled dusk.

We eat cuttlefish off the bone, from a secret
compartment in the hamper, roasted
over charcoal. A leopard's head
on the catwalk translates into sleek chic
ears on my snood, & an ivory-plated choker.
A light hooked to the flame.
Staccato stars.

Not far away, in a Bournemouth drawing room,
a wronged woman wrings her hands,
dips fists in rosewater & elaborates lists.
A screen in the corner shows classic Hardy
with round-vowelled milkmaids & joking
yokels. She'll bemoan her outdated life,
while half-attending to the muted drama,
& scribbling down names of dresses like *Milly-Joanne*.
Wouldn't it be better to think he had gone to war,
she'll flash in her tarnished cage.

I call him my "trumpet-major", enjoy
cut-throat frissons of Jurassic passion
& ask about her at intervals. *Ask her*
to forgive me. Here is no real light.
Only hard mouths, hands, & jungle
hunger – & knowing
that nothing, often, can be reversed.

TARN MACARTHUR

The Bone Caves

Inchnadamph

Back past the hatchery and sheepfold and waterfall
headed forward, eyes open, into the prehistoric.
Into the darkness that knows us from long before
we were us. Into the absence that homes us.
Where vision adjusts. And the shadow of a shadow
cast on the rock-wall is the flicker of a thought
escaped from the menagerie that brought us
where we are. Together. Holed up within the cliffs
above the Allt nan Uamh. Within the limestone
mausoleum. Bone reliquary. Amidst skeletal
remains of lynx and polar bear. Reindeer and wolf.
Bedded down in the earth for a touch of warmth
while the wind and snow white-out our tracks
and wherever we go beyond this point we go alone.

The Bone Trowel

A relic out of time and place. My grandfather, down in his garden rising and falling to the rhythm of work days before death, the bone trowel in hand. *This is us*, he said, scooping holes in the earth, half teaching me the work and half telling me the work is what you are. Hacked off and sanded down, the mandible of a pilot whale turned tool then heirloom, particles of dirt from St Kilda to Ontario carried in its calcareous cracks. I dropped seed after seed then tamped the soil with a child's attempt at solemnity, but what I really wanted was to ride on the tractor and listen to stories that from anyone else would have passed for fantasy – the myth of the huntress with her longbow and knives, or the tale of the House of the Faeries. We finished our work then went inside. One week later I stood at his grave while my father and uncles passed a shovel between them. Of course, death meant next to nothing to me then. So when they asked what I wanted to remember him by I picked up the bone trowel. Afterwards we must have stayed on for weeks. I saw my father cry. I watched as the living day by day grew from the touch of the dead.

The Lord of the Isles

Port of Oban

Not a cloud in the sky, still we're going nowhere.
Wind barreling waves down the Firth of Lorn
and the *Lord of the Isles* moored in the bay
till god knows when. This is what life really is.
Waiting it out in the same small town your father
did like his father and his. All the shopfronts
shuttered as if weather were the worst of our fears.
Deadfall on the tracks and the train like a relic
sits in its terminus. Salt-spray on the promenade.
Cold clockwork of seabirds winding the day
to little avail. Going nowhere, but they're going.
And up on the crest of Battery Hill the tower
stands like a Roman ruin with the wind blowing
through it. This time tomorrow might be different.

PAULA BOHINCE

The Skunk

A smolder, an echo of shame, the weary wick of it.

In the smudgy *Local* section, a fire living underground for half a century
will be put out. An ember tossed into a mine shaft
within a mile of my house, some midnight by a tired anonymous, that person
surely dead now, the consequence roaming since, low-lit
at times as a candle, other years ghost-vigorous.

I wanted to go to it, to feel the sorry emotion of it, the same impulse
in the therapist's office, the quiet "I don't knows" lodged there.

Mornings of fog, crystalline memories, and sympathetic roads.

I thought of the Italian modernist who was like a brother
the winter I again took up smoking to stand in the pristine and be
belled over. In one poem, he cupped a firefly, ember of childhood, for his mother
and ran home at breakneck speed to keep it illuminated.

I felt that. Exhausting myself, plugging every leaking aspect of myself
for her smile, to wake her, there at the table.
A flicker at the corner of her resisting mouth, and I went wild,
memorizing her the way others did 'Ozymandias'.

One Christmas, when I was grown, I wanted to cook for her
the meal of a lifetime. To say, "Mom, this is living. This is love. Feel it."
Flakes of salt on pursed lips of asparagus, duck
limp-necked on the second-hand platter.

She kept her head down and ate with shame, quickly, and gave me
before leaving melted together wedding rings, hers and my father's.

Amulet for I don't know what. Pain-medallion. Coin for the underworld.

In the New Year, I flattened beneath the dentist's lead apron
and thought of her (I am always thinking of her), her pilled red sweater, how she
looked around at the candles, her face scorched from crying.

O hiss of an iron releasing its malice, as I sat on the filthy floor, as she held it
to my ear, whispering, "Your father prefers the bars to us. He won't (*hiss*)
come home because he hates us."

What a paradise we could have lived.

Now, by the smoking hole, inflections of rain come faster. Visionary rain
and séance rain, sincere shawl of rain
as the skunk's wrapped in the shawl of herself, her offspring in the den
where tree roots are dead and it's pathetic to live so near.

Shovel-headed, digging into the past, I work, I collapse, I lie
on a vibrating mat meant to mimic the maternal embrace.
The TV reads me a lullaby of recipes in a voice soft as rain ceasing.

I sleep while the fire seethes through the maze.

"Conjure the perfect nurturer," the therapist said. He shifted when
I spoke an octave higher, when I cried out for "the mother's animal body"
and made a snuffling motion with my face, meaning I wanted to burrow
against it. Sometimes I did. Sometimes I placed her hand on my hand.

If I could build an ideal mother, calm in linen, in sedate earrings, would I?

Once, she appeared as Meryl Streep, in the field
where my real mother burned off her rage, and I was made to follow,
less than dog on a leash. In the therapist's office, among the smashed stalks,
breathlessness, sweat, Meryl said to me, "This sucks."

Tender skunk-mother, I love you, receding in your backwards shuffle.

The songbirds are gone, disavowing the hellhole soon to be filled with spring water or some alkaline compound: balm of man, cold compassion.

MARY JEAN CHAN

Calling Home
after Anne Carson

While talking to your mother you keep your fingers busy, your mind elsewhere. Her voice flows through your soul like air. Today you are sad, and she knows to ask about the tightness in your throat. After all that has happened, have you finally forgiven each other? The child asks: *How long will it feel like burning*. Your mother wants to know what you had for lunch, tells you what she ate for dinner. This mutual exchange of images. You ask her to turn on her camera, knowing she'd refuse. *Another day*, she says. After decades on earth, you should be able to know each other. All children want their parents to see them, as they already are. Instead, you are sent photos of yourself: an eight-year-old in a beige dress at a wedding, an awkward teenager dressed for the opera in Milan on your first trip to Europe. How to tell her: none of those versions fit anymore. Your partner walks into the room. You are reminded that you cannot change those you love most, your voice blue in the violet hour.

AMLANJYOTI GOSWAMI

Bus routes of childhood

Machkhowa: Fish eater.
Dighalipukhuri: Long pond. Not Silpukhuri: Stone pond.
Or Joorpukhuri: Twin ponds. Nak kata pukhuri: Chopped nose pond.
Ambari: Mango garden. Bharalumukh: Mouth of river.
Sharab Bhatti: Booze joint.
Adabari: Ginger garden. Near Jalukbari: Pepper garden.
Jorabat: Stitching ways. To the hills where the air turns cold.
Teeni aali: Three alleys. Saari aali: Four alleys.
Bijoynagar: Victory city. Swamped by the flood.
Barowari: Twelve come together (for a cause).
Pan Bazaar: Betel leaf bazaar. Books housed in childhood.
Aath gaon: Eight villages. Can't find any.
Puronigudam: Old godown. Near ma's place.
Palashbari: Garden of palash flowers. Dad's place. Khatiamari: Where the deer was killed.
Santipur: Place of peace. Near a hospital, a football field.
Nagaon: Nine Villages. Where ma comes from.

Bus routes of childhood. No place to sit, standing room only. On the ledge, breeze on hair.
Travelling tomorrow with yesterday's eyes.
Crossing fairytales along the way, but never knowing. Not paying a penny.
The bus stops at odd, dusty places, looking for memories. No passenger in sight.
Come one come all, the conductor screams.
There are no mango gardens, victory cities, villages left. They were gone when I came.
Ways no longer knit on their own.
The old ponds remain, feelings dip, mirrors face the past. Carrying sirens at midnight.
Once upon a time, there was no city. There were only dreams, gardens, a flower market.
And you still ask me, why do I like it so much?

Swing Quartet

Why Marshall appeared is still a wonder.
Salt-soaked, dipped in brine, hands gripping cherry
Lined with thread, a short run up,
And bursting in, with that pace

Straight at the helmet, or the stumps
Cartwheeling a few miles on, behind Dujon.
He had 376 when he turned up, grinning wide
Speaking a Bajan tongue, something like *there is more*.

And there were. Whispering death,
Holding, filed in smooth as a Rolls Royce,
Zipping past the pitch, and rolling the stumps or sending
Dujon flying, for another one-handed wonder.

At first change, Garner, beanpole who lurked
In the shadows, waiting for this moment
And when it came, lurched down the thick of battle
Landing it from 12 feet high, a javelin that uprooted the sticks.

Finally, slowly, lumbering, and yet as fast as fast can be,
Bearded Andy, soft-spoken, been there before, comes crawling in,
He knows how to stay the course, and on another day,
Would have led from the front. He is the best on his day.

That brings me back to Malcolm, of the wide smile, now gone.
Michael, Joel and Andy are there, reminiscing the old days
Behind a mike, inspecting pitches for signs of grass, wear and tear,
The odd bump, the little patch that would turn.

In their days, they needed none.
All they needed was a chance to swing an arm.

The other end did not matter.
The fearsome four, came together, hunted in pairs,

And when they were there, you didn't need a fifth
To complete the symphony, such was their charm,
And their sang-froid, their ease of spirit, their nonchalance.
It was almost boring to stand there

And wait for the opposition to do something,
Something else. Stare them in the eye, find some guts,
Turn the bat once and ask, if there was more.
Yes, Malcolm whispers softly, standing at the other shore.

STEPHANIE SY-QUIA

from *Amnion*

There was English, in the clerestory of my mouth. There was French, stowed in the front of my lower jaw.

My father spoke Spanish, which was slippery on the tongue and the teeth like a series of smooth stones.

And then there was German, that language my parents peddled between them like a secret.

When I was five I told my mother that American was a sideways language. French and English were perpendiculars.

Words are for things and some words are the truest possible expression of the thing. For instance: *vielleicht, gourmand, moist.*

French was a series of tight-skinned drums I needed to hit quickly in turn. English was round in the middle and sometimes closed, sometimes open, at ends.

There are some words that tether me more strongly to themselves and therefore the world. What do they do with their one inadequate language? What moors them?

My father spoke Tagalog until he was five. All that is lost now. He knows only the monsoon sounds of that season attendant upon his most unpromised birth. There is that lilt in it that sounds like the saddle of the afternoon, before the sky splits like the belly of a fruit.*

*Note how I could have said *like the belly of an overripe fruit* or *like the belly of a rotting fruit*. But to do so would have been toddling into the tintypes you draw on when you think of those places encompassed by the tropical clime as being stultifying, cloying in their fertility, somehow unclean even in that you see them as a possibility for plunder.

Did you know? That the colonised mass is often configured as female body – the Americas as luring one in and revealing their dangers later; Africa as dark and sinister and the utmost alluring in inscrutability. And in my meetings with people, often is the assumption that it is my mother who is the Filipina.
Please explain.

. . .

(Y)
I am the bracketed why
The W? XY said
I am the ɑ: u bet
the c u next
I am the body of the text.

I am the why
in French: Greek I
the lone line self
upright probe & pelvic cradle
splay me open for an X
mark the spot with sex
hang the sheets out to dry

Of Canterbury I recall
scuff
stone smell
shoe seep
smell at crotch of tights
"blazer".

The land seemed so old, but deluded also.
The white horse that leaps on the green hill, singing in chalk,
is a copy.

The stone of the cathedral came from Caen, where as a child in an oversized fleece
I stood in a very large crater near the Museum of Peace.
"My father was at D-Day and was shot in the hip, he lay on the beach in the surf
for three days." My godfather has my baby sister strapped to his chest.
This cool cold plain of Europe's beige edge is on par with Mont-Saint-Michel, its great flat-footed expanse where my brother and I dig its ridges for clams before the tide
comes running.

This is deep bone knowing country.

Albion.

I hold it in my mouth with pleasure like a corp
ulent pearl.
It contains all the story England tells itself:
a plosive, bounded space, girded by neat cliffs and land's end.
how they thought of their virgin queen,
the whole universe under her skirts.

The dean beckoned me and with his thumb
upon my forehead said *admitto te*
and I having for sole reference the Simba smudge, stumbled on the stiff white surplice lent to me on a two-year lease.

They were so blithe about the signifiers of their station. They had hairless pits and thighs, and paid, from the age of not yet fucking or fingering, for bikini waxes even though it was not, and would not be,

bikini season for some time. They had an easy greed and met me with
incomprehension when I tried in vain to explain where I came from.

My female hood was boarded over my eyes like a set piece. To determine
its deviance became the all-consuming aim. Cover your shoulders.
Shoulders remind boys of boobs.
My body became as incendiary as a vernacular.
It was the thing that lay in the dark woods at the trailing ends of sentences,
at the short edge of night and late at skirt.

The blonde others aspired to be described with mean, hard-nosed little
words: thin, pretty, nice.
I wanted big-femur words like wise and kind.

The boys were always
touching
each other.

I wanted big-beamed love. I wanted to be one of the women who swear
and have grey in their hair. I wanted, though this too was warped, to be
the emotional centre without which nothing can hold.

In our lesson the timelined people have made landfall in America. The
people they find there are untimelined, according to the landfalls they
have no history. This is something that even the ancients did not know.
This is something entirely new. Everything is uncertain. The world is of
unknown proportions. Luther is nailing a piece of paper to a door. He is
standing saying I stand before you now and can do no other. Everything is
chaos. Nothing is known. The universe is a black womb rioting with stars.

On the staircase in the history block was a framed print
    WE SHALL FIGHT THEM ON THE BEACHES
all around it dotted coats of arms and rays of light, which seemed a slight
confusion.

. . .

There is a word that appears only six times in our language, *banhus*
meaning bone-house.
This is called a kenning, a word not even 150 years old. It comes from
the Old Norse *kenna*, to know, to perceive. If I were to ask my mother
she would say that German *kennen* is for knowledge that is already
within, and *wissen* is for knowledge that enters. *Ken* is excused of
empiricism.
In Old English scholarship, a kenning is a compound word, but a
purposefully poetic one; it is a metaphor compressed. Thus a bone-
house is a body.
A house made of bones is like a great hall in the time before cathedrals,
beam-ribbed.

My body is a hall on a hill in the dark.

Give me a life of bleeding on your behalf!

I had teachers who nudged me towards the open hungry vowels of the
marrow-cracking class,
who woke me from the sleep of sixteen years and led me to literature,
which was a great fridge in the middle of the night and I was starving
(sixteen and straining in my pinstripes).

So I came to texts, and those who have been appointed to tell us what
they mean. I sympathised with those spined creatures we split open on
desks, discerning their dispossessed. Jesus was in everything; a bore.

At the school I learnt:
to twist praise and to deflect it always
that boys were *growing men* with *needs*
that I was disgusting and, at best, allegorical.

ANGELA CLELAND

I'm in Costa with the other new mums again

and behind our eyes we are all as desperate not to talk about this as we are to talk about it. The looped security footage of our birth stories, with their statistics, their metaphors, and their "home-from-home" decor, masks what is really going on in our corridors, where we are slipping past galleried rooms in which they are taking scientists, artists, nurses, poets, marketing managers and teachers and cauterising their specialisms, where we are sneaking onto restricted levels through doors signed "Nulligravida Only" in an attempt to break into a party in the penthouse where well-groomed women in backless dresses are discussing and postulating and theorising and conceptualising and there is a balcony without a handrail from which you can see the infinite possibilities of the night sky...

I'm in Costa with the other new mums again

and behind our teeth we are all struggling with the existential crisis brought about by giving rise to another consciousness. The looped security footage of our birth stories, with their lifts, their malpractice, and their operating tables, masks what is really going on in our corridors, where we are hurrying past blue-curtained berths where mothers are losing their minds to empty mirrors and blank photographs, as if it were a trade, mind for mind, mother for child, one-for-one, where we are sneaking onto restricted levels, through doors signed "Priests and Philosophers Only" beyond which we are certain there's a rooftop pool where a mind can exist in brittle solitude and know itself and be known, and exist in and of itself, where you can float naked and alone in contemplation without even having to close your legs...

I'm in Costa with the other new mums again

and beneath our skin we are all itching with bodily awareness. The looped security footage of our birth stories, with their waters, their faeces, and their haemorrhaging, masks what is really going on in our corridors, where we are slipping past rooms with blacked-out windows trying not to hear the screams or smell the freshly branded flesh, where we are sneaking onto restricted levels in an attempt to break ourselves out, through doors signed "Staff Please Ensure All Immunisations Are Up to Date", to the door behind which we are locked up and caged in and tied, gnawing at our shiny new bits, engraved with the words *I know what it is to be dead, I am meat, I am an animal in the wild right now; I know what it is to be animal, I am dead, in the wild I would be meat right now; I know what it is to be meat, I am an animal, in the wild I would be dead right now...*

NATALIE CRICK

Pearls for Little Girls

A gift for me, pale as an elephant tusk,
cut from the true moon's white skin,
shorn from the bones of stars in the sky.
I know you will wreathe me with them
like a Victorian bride. You will slip
this gift around my neck where you once
hung a thin candle. The flame touched the
constellation of my freckles funeral-
burnt. O wasp upstairs on the landing
I sense the lust you feel just now
looking for something to burn
looking for your own little girl pearl
to cut from her shell and polish
with hot blue bleach and I am charmed
to have loved you, O bad bad man upstairs.

HANNAH REGEL

The Deer Hunter

In the brief time that I was pregnant I watched everything related to Vietnam that I could find
It's war
All seventeen and a half hours of the Ken Burns documentary, *Platoon*, *M*A*S*H*, *The Deer Hunter*, *Apocalypse Now*, *Full Metal Jacket* et cetera. I was aroused and dumbfounded
By the men. Their rounded brown shoulders, quivering cigarettes. Dusty noses
I watched them all go to waste as I vomited into a mixing bowl on my second-hand sofa
I fantasised about being helicoptered into the fire. Nipple tassels swinging. A sweetheart

I would boost morale and in thanks be shown what sitting in a tank feels like. My neck
Would be held in a firm but tender grip as I am shown how to move the gun, looking into the viewfinder
"Like this, honey. Here."
I would sit on their laps and they would be thankful for the economy of my soft body binding us
Forever in the humbling of sex, how it makes religious animals of us all
Swigging from the bottle we would sing soft hymns about this quick shot at living
When we learnt how easy killing is.

WILL STONE

Opportunists of Genocide

Tank tracks still stitching their fold,
at dawn they emerged, dug over, sowed.
Those mud-slowed men moving west,
chins stained with apple juice and ash.
Someone smiling indicates the clearing...
Amongst lupins in flower they labour,
glean from the still moving soil
all they had gripped like charms.
At dusk the brimful wooden barrows
bobbed and scythed through the firs,
out of the village came wild dogs, the moon
found a silver comb owned by the girl who asked
of the barber, how long does it take to die?
She claimed it, plunged the teeth
into the woodsmoke waves of her hair.
Now caught out by the sun, the old one
steps quickly away from the past,
briskly brushing her strip of grass
of every intruding leaf.

Black Hole

In Siberia men of ash
move through the forest.
They know from childhood
every path and clearing,
where bee orchids signalled
and the sun spoke more tenderly.
Now they are hunted by predators,
wolf packs of flame that never tire
and their wives eat frugally alone.
Hard evidence has found us here
amidst the cold shell cases of science.
The pinioned sense the perfection
of the snare, searching beyond
meeting the dark eye out there.

DOMINIC LEONARD

The Going

I've begun no journey to speak of. Outside beats the night.
We, uncertain, stay. Nothing changes & hunger keeps.
We rule our holds. We grow up. We gave brave and wait for
The final hour which uses only flesh. I won't have fear
Die inside me. I'll attend to what crushes me down.
Strongest human quality is wanting not to die. To stay.
We agree, & waste our pain. Astonished one with the other.
It is just matter. Intended against us. I am sorry to mourn
Distant, grief barely to achieve its motion. In silence one
Tends towards that pedestrian weariness, in silence locked
Move closer. Knowing this gives you nothing. But no
Matter. Spring, rain-packed June – light & probability
& breadth sharpened on new-season angularity, stiffening
Fauna, long grass heaved bare, choirs of leaf rush, rains
Responding. & far from life the blood begins to slow, body
Creates body itself in bodies that shed that breath so far
From me. After a death there is nothing else inside you,
Bear it on. Easier then to form a different kind of thinking.
A disquiet. A fray. The night beating the object of the heart.
A necessary flaw, to take comfort in matter & its deliverance.
In the spirit, making its little motions. Mercy of this only life.
Someone years ago said nature has ordained one entrance
Into life but a hundred thousand exits. Hurts to say so
Many. I hold that that crushes me. The wind so loud. How
Can I sleep. Hence this work. Nothing changes. Hunger.
I'll go – where in the world, in its festival of winds – back
To my island, buffeted on by the breeze of this heavy going,
Thousands now.

Eclogue

The horses are dying.
We have been watching it for months.
Sad and tired, and most weak. I tell them,
Reality is hard enough without
Facing reality, pity
And no reprieve. No luck
No little moon of guidance. Bad
For the thimbleful soul. The grass
Pickles in the rain, heavy hedges
Gone sour; the wind blows the
Wind, whither it be
Gone to, what then. I show them.
They have left the river
Alone, now.
Locked out, sleeping
Their quarter of field.
The world stops at the field edge.
Beyond that it is not the world.
In the excelsis of slow almond
Snow, ajar and trembling their manes
Stop our hearts, their
Tin-strength, hoof-still. Everything
I have said I go back to. Everything I have
Written I put on the back of each
Horse. They bronzed and waned
And we buried them.

HAGIWARA SAKUTARŌ, *translated by Jae Kim*

Leaping Over the Earth

Certainly I do, have a special talent. But to *put it to good use*, there aren't any such special 'jobs' on today's earth. Rather, I would like to – to send the earth leaping far away, far beyond reach.

Fox

Look! He comes like the wind. The guest has greened from depression.
   Ears are sharply standing, ends of eyes are split in anger.
You! Where have you seen the likes of such beautiful expression as that which cunning draws?

Tongueless Truth

Inside a certain magic lantern, in a gentle, gentle landscape where bluish snow has fallen, I caught a glimpse of truth. Unable to speak and carry meaning, the sad 'tongueless' truth – I sensed it. Passing by the shadows of the landscape, the magic lantern, the piling snow, is a lonely blue cat, I sensed its figure.

Grave

This is a grave. Melancholic in the middle of wind and rain, sad and staying silent, lonesome and lonely, the earthy lump is forever.

What's under this grave? We don't even think about what's under this grave. Most likely a deep hole has been dug. So that a little bit of material – human bones, teeth, roof tiles – live together with a toad. Nothing's there. No one's life, mind, fame. No one who appreciates fame.

And yet look at us, why, so sadly, do we stand in front of the grave unable to step away? At any given moment in time, we believe in the nothing. The nothing remains. Our body decomposes and changes into other material. Ideology, sensitivity, emotion, that which recognizes the self, all vanish into thin air. Why would today's common sense accommodate that – that old-fashioned – superstition of the afterlife. We should think about the afterdeath and laugh like the wind!

And yet look at us, why, so sadly, do we stand in front of the grave unable to step away? We are unlucky artists, we hang tight against adversity. We endure solitude, we have posterity in mind, we're thinking of lasting fame. It's all we think about. Ah, but why does a person buried inside a grave make us self-conscious? We must live on. Forget posterity. Forever in the middle of the graveyard, we can't *not* stay alive.

Melancholic in the middle of wind and rain, lonely and silent for ever, the meaningless lump of earth exists. What's under this grave? We don't know. This is a grave! a grave!

The Poetry Society Annual Lecture Series

FACE – FACE – FACE

A Poet Under the Spell of Loss

Valzhyna Mort

When the Soviet empire fell, I was in fifth grade and attended a school that we, the schoolchildren, nicknamed Brest Fortress. The actual Brest Fortress is located on the western border of Belarus and is the site of the first major battle between the Soviet Union and the German Wehrmacht in World War II. The fortress was attacked without warning, launching the invasion of the Soviet Union. The Axis powers expected to take Brest in one day. The defenders, however, held out for days, which gave the rest of the country time to mobilize. Most of the defenders of Brest Fortress were killed or captured, while its defense became the symbol of Soviet resistance.

Our school squeezed itself between buildings with such other expressive toponyms as the actual World War II Museum, the Palace of the Republic, the Independence Square, and the military officers' quarters behind the People's Palace. War metaphors came easy to the generation that inherited world peace with an added bonus of national independence. We called our school a Brest Fortress because, without the right to defect, we had to exhaust ourselves until there was a figurative brain death in the building that resembles a fortification. For us, this was all a joke. "Well, who's laughing now?" I ask my schoolgirl-self across thirty years.

Not long ago, I sat down to write an essay about my former classmate Maxim Znak who is currently a political prisoner in Belarus. Max was a captain of my fifth-grade history team in our Brest Fortress, and today I think, with sadness and despair, about his ironic Belarusian journey: from schoolboy interested in history to political prisoner of a despotic autocrat. For the rest of the world, Maxim Znak is as if he really isn't – two one-dimensional words printed in the pages of *The Guardian*. For me, however, he is a face, a voice, a life. This is why when he was jailed, I felt beholden to tell his story.

In school, Maxim and I were friendly, but not close, so I worried I wouldn't have much to remember. Yet, I immediately recalled – to my surprise – Maxim's mother. I remembered his mother because that one and only time I saw her thirty years ago, she was reciting a poem. Not just any poem, but a poem built upon repetition. The line "Come on now, boys," which repeats from stanza to stanza, stuck in my head for all thirty years, thus proving its mnemonic worth. Maxim's mother recited this poem to us during a school assembly. A fifth-grader, I felt that by making me remember, the repetition was insisting on something, but on what?

In this poem, the Russian poet Yevgeny Yevtushenko talks about the cruelty of the young who come hard – "with sweaty fists" – against the mistakes of the old, while the old, with the baggage of their own mistakes, have grown soft, understanding. Here are a few lines from this poem in my straightforward translation:

> Come on now, boys.
> When we cease being cruel,
> we cease being young.
> Come on now, boys,
> but keep in mind that as you age,
> your cruelty will lessen,
> your empathy will enlarge.
> But other boys, arrogant and despotic,
> will come clenching their sweaty fists.
> Come on now, boys.

What does this phrase "come on now, boys" really ask of us? Sometimes, it seems to encourage the young men and express faith in male solidarity. At other times, it seems to question and mock. But what is it mocking: the cycle of violence, the forgiveness, both? What is the poet really saying when he repeats this address to the "boys"? How does he feel about the cycle of male violence and forgiveness? As the Soviet empire was collapsing around us, what was Maxim's mother saying to our schoolboys inside our Brest Fortress? Was she cheering on or warning? What could she anticipate about the violence to come? Come on now, what?

Thirty years later, her own grown-up boy – a former captain of a group of kids interested in history – would be making history as he was led, in plain daylight, into an unmarked van by the grown-up boys his age, their faces hidden under black ski masks. Hold the picture of these boys in your mind: they are the generation that inherited world peace with an added bonus of national independence. The growing ambiguity of the relentlessly repeated "come on now, boys" anticipates no escape from violence.

So what makes this poem mnemonic is not just repetition. Rather, it's the fact that with repetition, the repeated phrase grows more and more questionable. I've remembered "Come on now, boys" because, with every new repetition, it seems to offer more exasperation than encouragement, more doubt than assertion. I remembered this refrain because it kept me wondering about what it meant, which is to say, it kept me wondering about the kind of future it predicted. What is mnemonic about this repetition is not the reader's ability to remember it, but that the phrase itself remembers something about the people it addresses; it remembers violence.

Repetition, then, is not only a demonstration of something that keeps recurring: an endless supply of new generations of cruel boys with sweaty fists. It is also about our inability to stop this repetition: the established cycles of repetition are like spells and there's no anti-spell to stop them from happening. The more we repeat, the less power we have over the words and the more power the words have over us. Poetic repetition is about the potency of language and the impotence of its speakers. In our care, language is futile and change is impossible.

When I have to pick an example of the most potent poetic repetition that emphasizes the impotence of humans to interrupt it, I think of Paul Celan's 'Death Fugue', a famous poem set in the concentration camp. (Celan would get tired of the repeated publication of this poem, but here I am, unable to stop it.) Putting a fugue into the title, Celan sets up the structure of relentless repetition: in music, a fugue is built around the repetition of a musical theme in different voices. Each stanza of the poem opens with the return of a poetic theme, the key image of the poem – the drinking of the black milk of daybreak. "Black milk of daybreak we drink it at evening / we drink it at midday and morning we drink it at night / we drink and we drink" reads John Felstiner's translation. Three stanzas that follow all open with these same lines as the drinking becomes clearly forced, inescapable. At each stanza break, the white space between the stanzas offers a possibility of escape from the repetition of the deathly image, a hope that a new stanza will bring a change in imagery, a break in the forced drinking of the black milk. But a new stanza opens and the same image is repeated, closing like a trap over a fleeing, unpunctuated voice. The musical form of this repetition – a fugue – strips us of the possibility of using reason against the black milk, using words. The musical orders to drink are beyond our ordinary rhetoric.

Repetition hypnotizes, persists. It appeals to the potency of sounds to enact something not by accumulation but by driving a sound-pattern to nonsense, making it lose all confidence in meaning. Poetic repetition knocks on the doors of words, it demands that they crack, that they open. Repetition wants for language to be more than language can ever be.

Repetition creates a linguistic labyrinth where we get lost because every turn looks familiar – looks like a repetition – yet, instead of an exit we walk deeper into the spell of history. I'm shocked by this spell every time I write. A lyrical voice is a voice out of control and a lyrical poet repeats because she is shocked by what she said when she lost control of her voice. She repeats in hope that the words will come out differently on a second try, on a third try. She repeats because she hopes for a rupture of old patterns, a possibility of a truly new beginning.

The more I think and read about the history of violence in Belarus, the more I am confronted with such repetitions. For instance, when reading a book called *Belarusian Theater 1920–1930* by Andrei Maskvin, I became disturbed by the phrase "executed in 1937", repeated when introducing every single historical persona. The mention of every actor, director, or writer involved in the theater scene was accompanied by the date of their birth and death. Everybody was born in "year such-and-such", but nobody died in "year such-and-such". The tone of the book was formal, yet every new repetition of "executed in 1937" pushed the tone to the edge until it seemed nothing short of hysteria with a straight face. With each new repetition, the totality of executions grew and the sheer extent of it was impossible to handle with a matter-of-fact reading of a scholarly text. My reading experience turned into an anticipation of "executed in 1937". There was no other narrative but the narrative of these executions, with some details of theatre life to fill up the pages in between.

I remember a small pamphlet that fascinated me when I was a child. The pamphlet was dedicated to the defense of Brest Fortress, the actual Brest Fortress, not the joke one. There were about 8,000 soldiers in the fortress, and most importantly for me, about 300 families. The pamphlet consisted of photographs of the fortress defenders, with their names, date of birth and date of death written underneath. Under most photographs, the date of death was written like this: "tortured and murdered by the fascists during the siege of the fortress."

Amid the faces of officers, soldiers, cooks, and drivers, there were photos of children. Girls my age had a particularly strong effect on me. One of them, Nyura Kizhevatova, was "tortured and murdered by the fascists during the siege of the fortress". The photograph of this girl, along with the language describing her death, and the repetition of this language under many photographs, fascinated me. The philosopher Emmanuel Levinas writes about the Other whose face awakens us to the Other's humanity and to the profound differences between human beings. This awakening makes us beholden to each other. What made me feel beholden to Nyura Kizhevatova was her face, yes, but also her name. A name like Nyura seemed to belong to somebody full of life, full of girlhood, full of mischief. Somebody, unlike the officers and soldiers, like me. It seemed that "tortured and murdered by the fascists during the siege of the fortress" was a mistake in relation to this name, in relation to Nyura's face under a thin headband with a bow – a kind of a mistake one makes after having to repeat the same phrase too many times.

So I kept returning to the pamphlet and obsessively rereading it. My agenda was impossible: to knock on the words until they give in and change themselves. I opened the pamphlet and read because I thought that by doing this, I was giving Nyura a chance to survive. I hoped that a new reading would reveal that all previous readings were in fact misreadings. The only way of making sense of our history was to discover that it was all a misunderstanding. My rereading was a chance to reveal that death was attributed mistakenly, out of the inertia of mindless repetition.

Last year, my research kept bringing me back to the Belarusian villages burnt to the ground during World War II: 9,200 fire-villages, as I call them. Over 5,000 of them were burned down together with all their inhabitants, who were gathered in the largest building, usually a school or a barn. They were massacres, thousands of them in the course of three years. No mercy was spared for small children. People who tried to break out of the building were shot dead immediately. Today, Belarus has a museum-cemetery memorializing the burned villages. Online and in print, I've come across a list of their names – over 5,000 toponyms. The names of the villages that no longer exist stretch and deepen my idea of my country's geography and landscape. The film director Andrei Tarkovsky writes: "In a certain sense the past is far more real or at any rate more stable, more resilient than the present." Burned to the ground, these villages are never truly gone. They persist. What's gone are the names of the massacred people.

Most Soviet war monuments are dedicated to an "unknown soldier" and only people deemed heroes have the privilege of being immortalized in street names and monuments. In the poem 'Facing It' by the American poet Yusef Komunyakaa, a Vietnam War veteran reads the names of the perished American soldiers:

> I turn that way – I'm inside
> the Vietnam Veterans Memorial
> again, depending on the light
> to make a difference.
> I go down the 58,022 names,
> half-expecting to find
> my own in letters like smoke.

58,022 names written on a 500-foot-long wall! Known soldiers, with names written in stone in the capital city. I had to see the monument with my own eyes to believe it. The ideology I grew up with believed in numbers ("26 million dead") and cared for the names of the cities that needed to be defended, not the people defending the cities ("Moscow, Stalingrad"). "We will never forget" is written on war monuments instead of the names of the dead.

Out of over 9,000 villages, I was able to find the list of the murdered people only for a single village – the village of Khatyn, which has become the symbol of fire-villages. There were twenty-six houses in Khatyn, with 149 inhabitants in total. I return to the list of the perished Khatyn inhabitants the way one returns to a poem. The list of the dead looks like an elegy, where the names of people sharing the same house appear to form a single stanza. In each stanza, the family name is repeated as a full rhyme at the end of each line, from the grandparents' generation to the grandchildren's. Here's house/stanza number four:

Iosif Baranovsky	1899
Anna Baranovsky	1906
Nikolai Baranovsky	1928
Stanislav Baranovsky	1929
Vladimir Baranovsky	1931
Gennadi Baranovsky	1932
Leonida Baranovsky	1932
Maria Baranovsky	1933
Sofia Baranovsky	1934
Elena Baranovsky	1936

I cannot help but return to the list of the perished, reading it like this, family by family, house by house. This full rhyme emphasizes that whole lineages were gathered together, their last name repeated until nobody is left to continue the family legacy. Once I know the names of these people, they are present in my picture of the world. To paraphrase Tarkovsky: The dead are more resilient, more present than the living. As long as I know their names and share my breath with them, they are present, in some kind of a dreamscape, and only time is non-existent.

The repetition of the family name at the end of each line is not an identical repetition. As the year of birth next to the family name gets closer to the year of the Khatyn massacre, 1943, there are fewer and fewer chances for a single miraculous survivor. As with the book about Belarusian theatre, each repetition turns into a contraction, a regular spasm anticipated and dreaded. The tone is no longer about listing everybody, but about the horror of a list that refuses to stop. The horrific inertia of repetition.

Once the number of repetitions goes beyond our modern idea of a nuclear family, every new repetition is the shock of an extra person. Each extra person stretches the territory of my country, stretches and deepens my history, my picture of the world and my own lineage. Here's house/stanza number seven:

Kazimir Iotka	1896
Elena Iotka	1898
Maria Iotka	1925
Albert Iotka	1928
Stanislava Iotka	1931
Dominique Iotka	1936
Regina Iotka	1937
Stepan Iotka	1939
Yuzef Iotka	1941

It hasn't escaped you by now that these families were large. Children worked on the land from a young age and were born regularly, on account of the high chance of illness and early death. The high birth rate serves as a century-tested mechanism for a family's survival. This mechanism might be century-proof but it doesn't withstand a genocide.

Here's house/stanza number twenty-two:

Anton Yaskevich	1896
Elena Yaskevich	1895
Victor Yaskevich	1922
Vanda Yaskevich	1923
Vera Yaskevich	1924
Nadezhda Yaskevich	1934
Vladislav Yaskevich	1936
Tolik Yaskevich	7 weeks old

The last line in the stanza announces the death of the youngest child, who falls under the murderous inertia of rhyme and repetition. Everybody in this stanza/house has their official first name listed, but the name of seven-week-old Tolik is a diminutive. His full name would be Anatol. He hasn't grown into his full name yet, but the rhyme of his last name pulls him into the pattern of death. The names of the children – Vanda, Vera, Stanislava, Regina, Tolik – actualize them, turn them from a number – or, rather, from a number of extra hands on the farm – to a person named lovingly – for how else are such beautiful names given?

Thus, confronting me with her first name is the unknowable, yet real – because loved – Other. I'm in awe of the Other. I'm in awe of the fact that Nyura Kizhevatova existed, and the Baranovsky, Iotka and Yaskevich children also existed, and now I exist. I want for you to be in awe of the fact that Maxim Znak exists, loves history and jogging, and has been in jail for months. I know Max, but I don't know those children, perished long ago. Yet, every time I read their names, death swipes them into oblivion right in front of my eyes, and I become beholden to them. I have to breathe their names into the air with utmost love, this way I repeat them as they were in life, not in death.

Once I recognize Stasya, Regina, and Tolik as the Other, I start longing for them, for their faces and voices. They are now a part of how I imagine our timeless world. I recognize how incomplete my picture of the world used to be without them, and how incomplete it remains, filled with my longing for their faces and voices. Such longing accompanies my own family story.

By the beginning of the war, my grandmother and her siblings were orphans. My grandmother's older brother, Vaclav, got evacuated to Mordovia, where he, a teenage boy without food or family, survived the war. Then he came to Moscow to study to be a pilot, got pneumonia, and died alone. During those couple of years in Moscow, my grandmother and Vaclav wrote letters to each other. But, moving from the barracks to her first apartment, my grandmother lost the letters. I grieve the loss of these letters. I grieve that I cannot know Vaclav's face. The image of myself in this world could never be complete without his face, his handwriting.

My grandmother's younger brother, Boleslaw, went missing in Minsk during the first day of the bombings. She looked for him until she died. I also look for him, because I know his name and the fact that he was four when Minsk was bombed in 1941. I look for Vaclav and Boleslaw in my own face. The dead are stable, persistent, and I, a person without a home, rely on the dead as my most reliable community.

Without knowing the faces of my dead, I grew to see faces everywhere: a pattern on the curtains, on a napkin or a blanket seemed to be anthropomorphic, three-dimensional. My childish eyes saw traditional diamond shapes as garlands of anthropomorphic figurines that circled me and watched me go about my day. Years later I discovered that they are in fact the representations of Belarusian pagan gods and goddesses. A repeating diamond pattern is the motif of Belarusian traditional embroidery, which is a language of its own, a non-verbal one. Embroidered with red thread over white linen, the repeating pattern of Belarusian embroidery is a refrain, a chant that insists on good fortune, good weather,

Photograph © Georgi Likhtarovich

health, prosperity. In museums that specialize in traditional embroidery, scholars read an embroidered textile. I love to see such a reader follow the embroidery with her finger the way we do when reading a book or a musical score. The sun is the diamond with rays going out. The earth is a diamond with rays going in. Life is a diamond of the sun placed inside the diamond of the earth. By itself, it's just a symbol in an encyclopedia. The symbol gains power by being repeated. If a person is sick, the sign for life would be embroidered on their clothes and household linens, repeatedly proclaiming life – life – life – life. This repetition is as much a spell for the good as it is a representation of the claustrophobia of lives unable to escape the violent patterns of history, both national and familial; lives in constant need of good spells. At home, I cover myself with a blanket and a row of diamond gods lines up across my nose. Are they supporting or reproaching me? I look at them and wonder as they repeat, repeat, repeat.

This is a published version of The Poetry Society Annual Lecture given by Valzhyna Mort on 2 March 2021, the first in a series of lectures in 2021 presented by The Poetry Society in association with University of Liverpool (as the Kenneth Allott lectures). Further lectures in the series by Terrance Hayes and m nourbeSe philip will also be published in future issues of The Poetry Review.

SAMATAR ELMI

The Snails

I mean, the analogy writes itself
like the onion in a grand conceit
though we really are like two slugs
in a derelict mausoleum.
Google "snails are..."
Dangerous. Slow.
Destroying my garden.
Our jobs and our women.

You, who cannot speak snail,
wouldn't understand how the shell
was the gift and curse of diaspora,
how our songs and laments resound
in our half-remembered houses
that we carry to forget, to carry on.

VONA GROARKE

Linkage

The cure for loneliness is solitude.
– Marianne Moore

Rooks in the oak quicken on impulse, then flit
all over the place. I swear there's a pattern, if I knew
how to read it, how to breathe in sync. That was earlier,
coming in from the woodshed; now hard frost slicks

the roof tiles under which I try to sleep. I make out
stars I have no name for and the world feels empty
all of a sudden, like the oak when the rooks have,
as if on cue, pulsed once and again, then up and off.

But that's the world for you and no amount of opera
from the Met or thinking of whosoever you love
or used to do or want to do or cannot sets it right.
And that's before ever you get to rounding on the news

which isn't, would you credit it, so heartening these days.
It's got so it feels like switching on is opening the door
to a man in a t-shirt reading "I will shit on your mattress"
and inviting him in anyway, asking "Mint or camomile?"

It's got so it feels like every time I notice the sky
behind the oak, behind the rooks, is a wrong move.
Focus, *focus*, on what's to hand; beyond that is beyond
my ken; too abstract, sheer, for my slight imaginings.

Mostly I think that when I top a perfectly boiled egg
and eat it with bread I've made with my own two hands,
that might mean as much as photos in newspapers of men
in the back of pick-up trucks flourishing their guns,

and when I leave out fatballs for birds, that might be
roughly equivalent to, say, three sessions of therapy
with the guy who says, "You must set aside everything
and everyone you know, and start all over again",

and when I stop on the street to turn my face up to the sun
it will be the same sun, give or take, as the last time my face
angled to do this despite drone attacks and drive-by shootings
and wildfires and the whole school that slid clean over a cliff,

and when I plant bulbs in October and look forward all winter
to what they'll be, that might best the chump (pick a chump)
on the news, with a whole new way of reminding the world
it's his world now, not a damn thing we can do until he's done.

Truth is, that world doesn't deserve me or anyone I know;
that world in which strangers send dick pics to my daughter
and young women (any women) think the likes of Trump
worth their one vote. *That* world of men expecting "Please"

and "Thank You" with a "Yes, Sir" folded in, and outraged
when their well-upholstered innocence shows skimpy
held to honest light. *That* world of unbreathable breath,
of what's stacked so hard and high no glint gets through.

That world, shouting and shouting, glowering, finger-wagging,
all to remind you that, alone, you're not enough – not enough,
but still too much. What's needed is less *you* and, as a consequence,
less *me*. More silence and complicity. And to most of it,

I find I want to say either, "No Thank You" or "Are you for real?"
until the saying is a life (if I can get away with it). Not immune,
not aloof (I check in), but Jesus Christ, who can stomach the world
these days, when even Irish news has the words "body parts" in it?

Does saying No protect my innocence? Of course not.
Howsoever I position my body as shelter or sanctuary
I open cupped hands to find nothing but howl and glare
and an odd, angular emptiness too dry to live inside.

It's not much of an answer, granted, but it might be
what I've got and all I need, this fashioning of small rooms
into small civility; into this day's putting of a life on the line
that runs (does it ever run!) from rage to disavowal.

That the times are awkward is known even to a wind
that can turn corners, to a sun that outdoes itself.
And I, fixed between care and nonchalance, all the time
scrubbing off fixity and blanching decency, answer

with finding in a small life a space to breathe, and knowing it
for a luxury, and lining up words, these words, to call it so.
Is this redress or moral failure? Does it fail less uselessly
if I go hard at it, this solitude, determined not to flinch

or buckle, to withstand this day? To get through
to the end of it and tell myself: See, that wasn't so bad,
and if it didn't fall to me to rescue anyone, to help,
I did my level best to cause no injury, to be kind.

Fact is, you can't fix everything with paint and flower bulbs.
Sometimes the loneliness is too much; sometimes, the hurt.
Sometimes, it's just the being alive and having no answer
to the worst of it but time (which makes everything worse).

Or nearly. And yet. Bulbs do become tulips and snowdrops,
and today is a good day – no rain, no bills, no death to speak of.
If I'm lucky I'll sleep through the night and harm nobody
until I do, which is about all I ask for, these short days.

Quarantine

World dropped by at 3 a.m.
kissed my eyelids, stroked my hair,
said, "There, there; you're not alone.
I have other calls to make tonight
and every cell of skin I touch
I will ask to remember you."

And the wind said "Shush" through the keyhole
and the rain said, "Hush your lies."

But I wasn't listening in the least
with my hands brimful of stars.

ISHION HUTCHINSON

A Litany in Time of Plague

Brightness falls from the air. Nashe's error,
or what someone made Nashe's error, falls
on my ears in the bright afternoon,
laying waste to autumn, like elected
grace, long delayed this early November.
The vegetable garden is in seed.
Pandemic's work, and soon no more;
Lord, have mercy on us! Soon to be no more,
the blonde green lawn strokes of snow will blight
into darkness (*falls from the air!*) shining
off the executioner's instrument,
standing by as proof that old order
of song and counter song secures rapture.
Above all else, a garden can teach you
singing and silence the way it taught me
America, the bright cloven music,
whether incumbent or departing grief,
still totters on the scales of denial.

Les Murray's Bucket Hat

is a slack
pith helmet, a spaceship
shrunken above

his denizen grin
he flashed me once
in Bremen, his English

the dark gaps of Boethius'
cell, racked with
limpid Low German

on the radio. We were outside
the station, waiting to go up
when a breeze threatened

to lift the hat and I leapt,
not knowing how implacable
it was, as he, turning

an Olmec wink
to me, then ascended
the escalator to his voice.

MOHAMMAD S. RAZAI

Between the Latin graces

It was sometime in Michaelmas. Your face appeared flattering-pale in the tenebrous air of the Formal Hall like a consumptive's. Above your head – its aureole a champagne blonde – was the foot of Christ on the cross, the one you told me was oil on canvas. My side of the hall was darker still, but our eyes searching for each other met several times as the evening wore on. Under my intense gaze between the two Latin graces you grew paler. Cor cordium… you were everything I desired. I self-mockingly muttered O lente, lente currite noctis equi! I pretended it was a pompous jest, but I actually meant it. That evening, that term and many other terms passed until you left. I was just foolish to think time would be kind, stand still. I was eager to impress. I spent it jabbering about moral philosophy, Wittgenstein, when I should have told you about the sail, the storm, drowning.

Hazaristan

In a pure Hazaraghi tongue – lyrical like the songs of mountains – she croons, and her body undulates in the wind, rhymes with the fields of wheat and barley. Above her a cumulus rests dream-like low almost touching her embroidered cap and its silver Silsila. At dusk she corrals the oxen and the flock *baaing, maaing, mooing*, their udders bulging, teats engorged, the clay pot fixed between her calloused feet as the spurts of milk make high oscillation plinks. She churns it in a goatskin, the mashkh rolls, dances under her hands and bangles on the kilim – with each turning *whush whush* the solid leaves the liquidy milk, she scoops out the butter leaving in the buttermilk. Then, like a gallery that closes, the village plunges into darkness, the welkin bursts into light, distance melts, and even the distant one winks. This place becomes a Bluebeard's house, her glassy bangles break.

BEVERLEY BIE BRAHIC

Stylebook

Spelled with a 'u'
Colour
Has more colour

Than *color*
Spelled without
A slight flavour

A *je ne sais quoi*
Of the baroque
As misbehaviour

Might flatter
The neighbour
Holding the door

To the elevator
Cage on 2
A dapper silver-

Haired charmer
Who spells ardour
With a you.

Vanity

My eye encounters hers
In the treacherous glass.
Don't need makeup, she frowns
As I rummage a bag
For the leftover tubes
Of seductive names
Incognito, Scarlet Letter
Cunning pots of paint.
See, I cajole, how *Fauve*
Enhances your eyes,
How a glint of *Twilight*
Deepens their mystery?
She steals a look in the
Utilitarian
Glass, and relates again
The afternoon a man –
Younger man she emends
For the sake of precision –
Wanted to pick her up
In the gilded lift cage
Of that foreign hotel:
Istanbul? *At my age!*

A Dream Catcher

I gave the child a dream catcher
An orb of yarn and beads
And fluffy pigeon feathers
To hoop above her bed;

And in unsteady, rainbow-coloured
Letters on sky-blue paper she wrote
Back, "Thank you for my dream catcher
I think it's working."

MARIANNE BORUCH

I Could Redact Most Parts of Me So Memory

can't even reach them. I could, and really once
in Tasmania it was *you guys*

nearly off the map! our son wrote,
half mistaken-amazed as old cartographers in love
with vast, with a lot of water
around something, inking a three-headed dragon
to the corner.
Most didn't much leave their rooms.

Any nearly
equals beginning. Leave it to a map
to un-map. O cloud of close-your-eyes...

Hang on, said the sweet earnest boy
secretly writing his novel, selling us a printer
at Officeworks in Canberra
to over and over, the way

myth works any real story come along.

Real story: a fire about to be triggered
by ghost-gums and lightning.

Or floods that overwhelm. Or such beautiful days.

I understand, I said to the Indigenous Elder.
No you don't, he said.

. . .

The quiet, the way a kangaroo
stops, stared at me, its little
T-rex arms frozen for how many minutes.

What I mean is –
I don't know what I mean.

In an elevator the body aches for gravity as that
smallest room of the house rises like
some weird high-handed helium's in charge of
armies and ships, childhood, history,
future's next day to next, major exports and imports
of whatever time, place, race, gender we get

jolts to a stop.

Look down while you're up there: alley and meadow,
the town dump crazy-winged with gulls,
minor royalty in the kingdom
of old mattresses, busted toys and shopping carts
no matter how inland.
But everywhere is inland when you know
how far the sea drops dark at
edge of things.

Sea as idea, as Original Vague Rumor of Blue some
stranger had of water in the year of great fires.

Which year and whose year and how many years.

He walked away into
a little dot and spoke like a prophet.

I saw a mob of those dots

on the horizon most mornings –
Kangaroos! Joeys! More kangaroos!
I lifted my binoculars.

I see them too, big shot, an Archangel said in passing.

. . .

What is a moment if not this:

I am feeding a joey [stop]
in the bush capital [stop] *9,647 miles from home*

But a wallaroo in it! Low table, a couch, overstuffed
chair and chair high above the city. One window,
a door, four walls.
I repeat: a wallaroo in it –

People said lovely so often it *was* lovely.
And *brilliant* half the time
to advance the cause of Yes and Okay, subspecies
of Pleasant. Or was it
Phylum of Good Will,

Order of Forgive and Give Way,
Genus of Kindness or Grace or Smokescreen –

No Worries. No Worries. We'll get it sorted.

Stories got told: *I took one to work, tucked in this,*
this shirt. The big meeting went on, that dodgy invoice
they talked of but I could feel him there.

Vague rumor of blue,

a prophet who walks into *desolate*, into a dot.

A paw to his face like a cat, tidying up. Then curled as a leaf,
a wallaroo in my arms sated as far back
as milk is, as sleep is.
Historia Naturalis, according to Pliny.

KIT BUCHAN

Kind of morning

To wake, my God, the joy of it,
and to kind of see the day as you surface into it,
not looking round, not drinking down,
but sort of seeing it all the same.

And that day to offer up its gifts in ambience
so gradually, that I might go around collecting
like a stick wheeling in the floss,
and only in retrospect to know how sweet.

To go, say, down the stairs in wrinkled leggings
and find the two rooms filled with light, to stand
my lifelike face to study in the glass
while urine roars gladly in the bowl.

How fine and mental is the kitchen, then,
like the cockpit of an underwater plane:
the pots of seeds, the amber bulb above the rings,
the cold cans humming in the salad drawer;

and if anyone else is there, absolutely,
and they as well want quietly to sort of go
through the few rooms in our same leggings
kind of seeing the grey light lifting,

kind of seeing the walls, the shining face,
the lifelike face of this low, grey computer
a living organ in the obedient rooms
thinking clearly its loyal thoughts;

in fact to lie this way, even among others,
with the day pressing gently on our ears,
smoking and gazing fondly at the screen
as the day spirals down outdoors;

spirals down and crashes, sinks away.
Blows out and smokes like a spent match.
Crushes its red face against the glass
like the bottom of a glass ashtray;

and then to sleep, my God, the sleep of it,
and let the day wake around me as I lie alone,
until the day is burning around me like cool paraffin,
when then to rise and, sort of, see it

HELEN FARISH

Encounter

Beds of white tulips; a crow
on a high wall, wings
worn like a matador's cape;

from the sleep of a glass
bubbles rising; a mulberry
opening its lace of shade;

girls wrestling down
the sudden heat; the river white
at the weir, the roar saying

no, not here, not here,
the train saying don't board yet,
the pavement chair willing

its occupant to leave
so it could be the one
I'd choose from thousands,

the sun a stranger, disguised
as something grander than itself,
something splendid

colouring the air copper
with red feathers
at the borders of sight.

Turn your head this second,
says the crow. I've prepared you
for beauty, say the tulips.

Open, says the mulberry.
Rise, say the bubbles.
How can you be shy

at your age? ask the girls.
He just happened to be passing,
just happened to be walking by.

Woman with Red Bra

A crystal dangles from the central bow.
From behind, her hands on the sides of the cups,
the assistant says, "This label, *Marie Jo*,
knows how to shape the breasts, to round them up.
When it comes to lingerie, it's always the French
who have the edge. And life's too short not to own
a red bra, though you still get people who judge
women wearing this shade. Let me bring Joan
to double-check the fit." Is it too late
to sell up, move to Montmartre, a studio
in which I paint night and day? A clean slate,
an accordion in the rain, a high window.

Muse

With you, I was Picasso
pulling Dora Maar
up out of his soul,
taking her apart, rearranging her
time and again, the need
to re-engage, to see
what happened if I looked at you
with one true eye,
the other gone walkabout, prey
to dreams, distortions.

Now, I'm bespectacled Bonnard
gentle with his muse – Marthe
in the mirror, on the bed,
in the bath, in yellow,
her skin apricot, eyes grey,
her nipples orange, kohl,
then chocolate-blue.
And if I wake wanting you,
it's only the old marsala-dark
painted between my thighs.

TARIK DOBBS

the true american *wishes to be well-liked at the ford river rouge plant*

after shane mccrae

when the foreman calls   he names me
al   he says *it's good al*   *ford takes*
his chance on you   me   *but why are we*
paid the same   he laughs   but here
i try to forget all   to be well liked
in the plant   i take al   as my wife says
there are 99 names of allah   we don't
dare break for prayers   at first i'd salah
in the backyard   but michigan is muddy
usually   at ford's picnic i make a small
explosion   spilling my beer in the grass
the foreman's wife says   *god bless you*
              dear   allah has many names
but hu didn't know   this small death

the true american *will enjoy man's best friend*

my son is now three he has
inherited my great fear of kalb
sometimes in the car i see one &
pull faster i wish my imam was
here the great thing about islam
is i become my own imam i sing
about the dogs mostly for protection
beware dog i guess the men say this
my best friend & i learn to let it sniff
my hand i think ya allah my digits
could go like that but its nose soft
its gentle pull moving itself closer
much like i stepping off the boat
for that first time i cannot bite
the hand that feeds me my son
he wraps himself around my leg

GAIL McCONNELL

from *The Sun is Open*

BEGIN WITH VICTIM on his
back is how this could begin
place your mouth over his mouth
pinch his nostrils shut easier to
take what I have found and break
it up breathe steadily till victim's
chest begins to rise pause
every minute to glue it back
the wrong way take a deep breath
yourself if there is no air
exchange do not touch him

•

how did we spin the thread
that tethered each to each
me you you me how did we
exist before these letters all
these sounds I know sound we
had enough to sound out the line

between us

I had a sound for you by it I
called you daaaaaaaaaa deeeee
you had one for me the name you
gave me between one and two
syllables geeeaaaal you called me
your twice-voiced dawwww ter

•

he left
the vertical went from | to –

a changing shape a fall a turn 90
degrees I look up vertical it turns
to vertex the apex the crown
of the head a whirlpool
swirling into avert turning
his head my mother shouting
BILL turning it towards what
was coming

•

we burned the boats we burned
the sweets we burned the
packages they came in burned
the leaves along the path we
burned the bits of paper dropped
on pavement slabs we burned the
sign that said wet paint burned
the grass and then the edges
of our shoes we burned our laces
at the ends the plastic melting as
they frayed we burned a tract left
on a bench we burned the
matches in the box then burned
the box the matches came in

•

MY FATHER REJOICES
that's what it means my name I
mean but did he

what if anything
was the source of his joy

was there joy between
us

before he left or after he walks
through the hall the squeaky
door saddle across the tiles
walking outside into the morning
into those bullets sailing through
the blue air into perforation into
a heap into gravel an almost
human shape into death into
silence or whatever

comes after

•

O Father
my father
my Father in Heaven
Father with his angels

my Father is always working
Yes, Father
No one knows the Father
No one goes to the Father

bury my father
only Father

My Father has given me all things
every plant which my Father in heaven did not plant

O Father
my father
my Father in Heaven
Father alone
who remains in me

RICHIE McCAFFERY

Sawdust

The woods I walk border a timber mill –
all day long the pines listen to their own
being cut with buzzsaws into lesser forms.

The forest's revenge is to remain silent
which is the sound of all human effort
cut down to nothing by non-existence.

Sermon

In the churchyard the red admiral
lands on the wall where I'm sitting.

It has a clear sense of what it wants –
to perch with wings closed in a namaste

but the gun-in-the-back wind
keeps prising it open like pages

in a book before the spine's broken.
The stained glass of its wings

takes me into the church where
a bible with hinges completely cracked

is spreadeagled on the lectern
at the same old passage.

Only my father attends service here.
Once I asked him what the sermon

he had just sat through was all about.
He'd already forgotten. His brow

a tilled field until it came to him
in a harvest. It was about joy.

Interview

ALICE NOTLEY

Erkut Tokman talks to Alice Notley

Alice Notley was born in Bisbee, Arizona in 1945 and grew up in Needles, California in the Mojave Desert. She gained her BA from Barnard College and MFA from the Iowa Writers' Workshop, and was actively involved in the New York City poetry scene in the 1960s and '70s. She published her first book in 1971 and has written over forty books to date, among them How Spring Comes *(1981),* The Descent of Alette *(1996),* Mysteries of Small Houses *(1998),* Disobedience *(2001),* Grave of Light: New and Selected Poems *(2006),* Culture of One *(2011) and* Certain Magical Acts *(2016). Although Notley is often associated with the second generation of the New York School, she prefers to declare herself independent of all classifications. She married the poet Ted Berrigan in 1972 and they had two sons, Edmund and Anselm Berrigan, who themselves both became poets in a rare example of a poet family. After the death of her first husband Notley married the British poet Douglas Oliver in in 1988 and moved to Paris in 1992, where she still lives. Her poetry is narrative, meditative, epic and feminist, notable for its exploration of style and form. She is the recipient of the* Los Angeles Times *Book Award, the Griffin Prize, the Academy of American Poets' Lenore Marshall Prize, and the Poetry Foundation's Ruth Lilly Prize, a lifetime achievement award. Her most recent book,* For the Ride, *was*

Interview

Alice Notley

published in 2020 by Penguin.

I met Alice Notley for the first time in 2018 in Timişoara, Romania, at the LitVest festival where we were both participants. Over the following years I became more familiar with her work and we developed a friendship and correspondence, out of which this interview emerges.

ERKUT TOKMAN

You once commented, "Writing poetry is what I am. I wouldn't know what else to be." When did it first occur to you that you had such a special relationship with poetry, that it was your destiny?

ALICE NOTLEY

Hard to say. I began as a fiction writer; my first intentional works of art were short stories written while I was an undergraduate at Barnard College in New York. I read poetry and liked it, but it never occurred to me to write it as I was starting out. I still don't know why. But when I arrived at the Writers' Workshop at the University of Iowa I immediately met young poets and immediately began to write poems. I wasn't sure, for a year or two, whether I was a fiction writer or poet, and my degree, my MFA, was in both fiction and poetry. I found poems more fascinating to work on, and fiction more fictionalized, made-up. Fiction is a veneer of life – it's fictional and I don't believe it or have any use for it but as escape from my mind. Poetry seems much more beautiful, truthful, and monumental to me. I don't really like characters, plot, and so on. I do like dialogue, and there's a lot of dialogue in my poems. Also I have characters, plot, and so on in my long poems, but ruefully.

ET

How did your friendship with Ted Berrigan and Anselm Hollo at the Writers' Workshop in Iowa in 1967 influence your writing and your poetics prior to the publication of your very first poetry book, *165 Meeting House Lane*, in 1971?

AN

I met Anselm first, in 1968. He was this rather wild but also totally cultivated Finn, extremely well-read, who (like Ted) was eleven years older than I was. I've never been sure what his influence was or is on my writing, though I know it's there. We were always friends, and I am still flattered that he chose me as a friend. He liked my first poems, though I couldn't see much merit in them, and so he encouraged me. He liked things. He liked me. Ted I met about a year later – I took a break from Iowa, lived in San Francisco then traveled in Spain and Morocco. When I returned to Iowa City in early 1969, Ted was there, and he and Anselm were, amazingly, new friends. Ted was the catalyst, really, for my choosing poetry. I read his books, I listened to his talk – he talked a lot, and I followed his suggestions as to what I might write or write like in order to become myself as poet. My first book, *165 Meeting House Lane*, is a sonnet sequence influenced by the *Later Sonnets* of Edwin Denby. At that time they hadn't yet appeared in book form. Ted was staying at Rudy Burkhardt's loft in New York, found them in a closet, secretly photocopied them and gave the copy to me – we were living on Long Island – and I proceeded to imitate them. I found myself, through the act of imitating someone else's voice and form, dredging things up out of myself to say that I would never have previously thought of. Afterwards, I always sought to recreate this experience, though I eventually stopped imitating others.

ET

You don't see yourself as being part of the second generation of the New York School, and you've objected to your writing being pigeonholed as autobiographical, political, primarily concerned with addressing sexism, focused on motherhood, and so on. You once stated, "I serve the poem, no one." So what is your poetry bound to? Do you see your poetry as a corridor, with doors opening up into multiple rooms that you have never inhabited but only passed through? In the same way that you have never been part of a poetic movement but rather a visitor. Is the disobedience of your poetry a form of rebellion against existing rules?

AN

Poetry is an ancient, ancient art – a first art, unlike, say, the novel or film. People must need it – I guess I must think it's crucial to people's existence. When I began writing poetry, and for many years afterwards, I just asked of it that it let me get better at writing it. I tried out a lot of forms, procedures, and tones of voice. I wanted to be able to do everything it is possible to do in poetry. Now I think I'm really looking for where poetry might be most crucial to everyone's knowledge and also pleasure. To do this, I rather often have to go against what people think it is. The mainstream of poetry is always stuck in some past version of the form and of things to say in poems; I refuse to be stuck in any past version of it, even if it's a recent past version and is what my supposed generation does. I don't have a generation when someone's reading my poems, they're reading them right now in the moment of reading. They're not thinking about literary history.

ET

You once said this in a lecture on Allen Ginsberg's poetry: "There is only one interconnected, possibly damaged world." You continued by asking, "But who is saying kaddish right now for the dead of Ghouta? (March 2018) in Syria, abandoned by America and all the world." You went on to quote William Blake, who famously proffered: "we are led to believe a lie / when we see with, not through, the eye." In your own poems you cry out, "I want this economic and political structure to collapse soon / that will be so painful for us / As painful as mourning is?" (*Certain Magical Acts*). How do you perceive this clash between art and politics in our post-truth era? Do you think the poetic act can gain the kind of role it had for the Beat generation or at the time you were an editor for *Chicago*, *Gare du Nord* and *Scarlet*?

AN

I don't think poetry and politics clash necessarily or even at all. In my poetry I usually let in whatever's going on in the world or universe, and so I have to let in politics or social problems or the behavior of governments, but I do this in the language and form of poetry, including the actual speech of living people. What I don't believe in is separating things or people or topics or situations from each other. I never have, either in politics or my life. My poetry and existence are very impure. When I was an editor, I published whatever I liked really; though sometimes it felt necessary to shout, particularly as an editor, since a journal is a somewhat public place. But I write whatever I feel like writing. My politics are never conventional, they adhere to no systems or parties, they aim at love, which dissolves all the names of such things into more beautiful formations and feelings. I learned from Allen Ginsberg, and from Ted Berrigan, and Doug Oliver, and my parents, the possibilities inherent in accepting and liking people; I aim for a more relaxed and genial existence. And I have said Kaddish in my own way, in my poems, for the recent dead of Syria, because it felt so necessary. Because my poetry cares for people, more than I am capable of as a person in daily life on the streets of Paris. I have my poetry to care with.

ET

In their analyses of the era of the New York School and the St Mark's Poetry Project, some critics have underlined the role of women poets, claiming that this has previously been underestimated or even neglected. What do you think of this view? Was sexism a salient issue?

AN

Sexism was certainly there, everywhere, when I started writing and trying to publish. I was born in 1945 so I am one of a first-ever group of women poets in the United States and there was a tremendous effort necessary on my part. Basically I had to convince all the male poets to pay attention to me and see how good I was and let me into their poetry world – for it was certainly theirs. I had no trouble with men like Ted or Anselm, but there were plenty of men who didn't want women to be there as practitioners, as equals. The territory of poetry, the material everyday power positions related to it, are quite limited, since poetry doesn't figure at all in the greater economy or money world. And nobody likes to give up their hold on things. Luckily for me I'm not interested in that power part, but I do want wider publication. And I did want to be seen for my talent and achievements, which at that time could only be seen through male or male-dominated eyes. All of this has been rather trying, though it's better now.

ET

You have said, "Society is a huge cohesive emotion; I can extract myself from that emotion for moments." What do this cohesiveness and your desire to extract yourself from it bring to your poetry?

AN

The truth! and better language. If you can stop thinking in society's language and feeling society's supposed feelings, you might actually be able to write some poems. Poetry exists in a parallel reality, perhaps the realest reality. At the moment I'm being told by both media and my friends to hate Trump, for example, but I don't feel like hating anyone. I don't feel like being inside the social detestation process.

ET

What do you see as the most contradictory and the most powerful aspects of your poetry?

AN

I suspect my poetry thrives on contradiction, which is simply a linguistic idea. I don't know if there is such a thing as contradiction outside of language. Poems are certainly made of language but would seem to try to resolve contradiction by placing contradictory elements next to each other in a state of friendship or love, no? The most powerful aspect of my poetry is probably how it changes your body and mind when you read it aloud.

ET

I can't stop reading your line "I'm the singer of tales of / bliss and structure of universe yet unperceived." In fact, it may also be one of the best ways to describe you. I perceive you as a modern thinker who philosophizes wisdom within poetry, and another critic has dubbed you "the Homer of our time". What can heal the poetry of today?

AN

Poetry heals, as I just indicated, by getting deeply inside your physiology and psyche and changing you. This happens most purely when one reads it aloud. My poetry can change the way you see things, and change the way you feel – can make you feel better or more interested or even smarter. But you have to give it a chance to do these things. It can make you be so much more interested in something besides yourself that you forget your problems long enough to calm down, without stirring you up in a phony emotional way like music or pretending that the world exists in a such-and-such way like novels. The world isn't really there like that, and if you forget about the version you've been trained to participate in, for long enough, you might suddenly "come to" in a different world. Poetry performs changes through a very peculiar use of language that exploits its minutest parts – sound, meaning, as they too are composed of little tiny particles that change into minute bundles of waves, and so on. We are all quivering, and our bodies are in motion as we sit still. We have decided we have boundaries, each, but do we? My poems quiver and make your mind and body do the same.

ET

You are the mother of two sons who both later became poets, and your two husbands have been poets. With this family milieu and various circles of poets, you managed to create a magnetic field that stretched across different cities and cultures. What was it that magnetized all those people from different generations around you? What was, as it were, the magic behind the scenes that raised the curtain between you on the stage and the audience? Do you remember any particular unforgettable or untold moments in that process?

AN

I think we as a small group have been magnetizing because we all care so much, or in the case of the dead did care, about poetry. We cared about other people's poems as well as our own and were open perpetually to a discussion of poetry and the other arts. We were and are open. Also, of course, we have talent, what one might call an objective sense of how words and parts of words relate to each other to sound out unpredictable but recognizable meanings that are also pleasurable. But meanwhile, I have secrets and intend to take them, as they say, to my grave.

Essay

SILENCE, SOUND, CEREMONY

The Poetry of m nourbeSe philip

Jason Allen-Paisant

A defining feature of the work of Trinidadian-Canadian poet and essayist m nourbeSe philip is its concern with sound and silence. These themes relate to the exploration of Atlantic slavery and colonialism: heinous, inaugurating experiences of the African diaspora.

For philip, sound and silence evoke body and language as intertwined concerns. How has the erasure of the languages and stories of enslaved Africans and their descendants worked to produce an ontological erasure of their bodies? These questions span the arc of philip's work from the early poetry and essays in *She Tries Her Tongue, Her Silence Softly Breaks* (1988) and 'A Genealogy of Resistance' (1997), to the book-length poem *Zong!* (2008).

philip's work insists on the need for Afroic people to "create, control and [...] understand their own i-mages". "I-mage" is her term for a language that speaks to "the essential being of the people among whom and for whom the artist creates". In the essay 'The Absence of Language or How I Almost Became a Spy', she writes that, "in stripping [the enslaved African] of her language, in denying the voice power to make and, simultaneously, to express the i-mage – in denying the voice expression, in fact – the ability and power to use the voice was effectively stymied". Her dissection of the English language serves to highlight precisely this. It is an attempt to retrieve traces of the poetic "i-mage" through picking English apart, and through the revival of an African sound. An African sound conveys the speech patterns of ancestors, the rhythms of their music, and echoes of rituals.

philip's poetry forces the reader to pay attention to notions of silence and sound. Line breaks are often like ruptures, syncopated drum beats. They emphasise rhythm and the breath. In this way, the poems achieve a sense of physical communication. The reader is not meant to be a mere receiver: they must become a performer in the reading. Repetition is important, carrying the resonance of Caribbean speech, and creating pathos, drama, emotion:

4.
oh for a race of women
mashing the ground
as if!
they owned it
not like he does

5.
to move
leaping from occupying space to
occupying the idea
the thought
to make it your own
taking up
more & more

6.
the force of baby
forces
you to
take more
& more &
more...
space

('As If')

"To speak another language is to enter another consciousness", notes philip in the 'The Absence of Language', which articulates the motivations behind her poetic project. philip wants to shine light on that sense of otherness that comes from the imposition of another tongue, but more particularly, to recreate for herself and her readers the sense of alienation experienced by the enslaved African who is violently displaced from their language through slavery. And this alienation becomes particularly poignant when the twin realities of being Black and female are considered.

how does the poet
how does the poet
how does the poet
"confront"
how does the poet
"loss and absence"
how does the poet
an absence of language
resolve

She doesn't. She listens to the silences\s— the interstices of time;
she listens
again
[...]

How does she
how does she
how does
she
      break
that silence
that silence
          is one
          is many
how does she break
one into many

('Ignoring Poetry')

We note the stops and starts, the interruptions, the recursions; the impossibility of smooth forward movement, of a sense of security in the language; the sense of an incommensurability between language and being. The poems are marked by the inability of language to coalesce, to contain the experience, to contain the body. The voice is forever indented. Language is always an insecure place. The language of the poet performs this insecurity, the recursion of past and present, of the past *in* the present.

Yet, at the same time, the poet is trying to retrieve an ancestral language, an ancestral mode of being, to renew connection with an ancestral conception of body, Earth, and world. She is trying to find her way out of history.

To be displaced from language is to be physically displaced. Yet the answer to this alienation, insofar as there can be one, is and must be poetry itself. So the poem is reconceived as *corporeal habitation*. Corporeal because it embodies its subject matter; corporeal also in that it places the body in action. The poem is no longer an object; it is a space of gathering(s).

body must remember song and drum
story and tale
how it was
how it stay
and how it wasn't/
[...]
body must remember the reign of life
and death
that body is not thing
and thing not body
must remember how we knew
and what was
knowing that knew and
knew not
finite end

('Meditations')

As a ritual of remembrance, a ceremony for the unburied dead, the much celebrated long poem *Zong!* is also a space of gathering(s). The entire work relies on text from the transcript of *Gregson vs. Gilbert*, the court case more colloquially known as the *Zong* case.

As the 'Notanda', philip's essay that accompanies the poem, explains, the *Zong* was a fully "provisioned" slave ship which, on one of its voyages in 1781, left the West Coast of Africa, bound for Jamaica with 470 enslaved Africans on board. Due to navigational errors on the part of one Luke Collingwood, the captain, the journey of the fateful ship is significantly lengthened (some four months instead of the usual six to nine weeks), leading to the death of a large number of the captive Africans onboard. Sixty people are lost through illness and lack of water; forty others "through thirst and frenzy" throw themselves into the sea and are drowned. Reasoning that if he threw the remaining "cargo" overboard, he could claim compensation from the insurers, the captain of the ship casts one hundred and fifty souls into the sea. Upon the ship's return to Liverpool, the insurers, Messrs Gilbert, refuse to pay out. A court battle ensues. The transcript of the judgement is the sole historical record of this heinous event. In the words of philip, "there is no telling this story [but] it must be told".

But how can the story be *told*, without *one* telling it? This can only be achieved if the dead themselves are allowed to speak. No authority, no "right words" can function here. Instead of using language, the poet must allow language to lead her. Only in this way might the dead be allowed to speak. Only in this way might a ceremony be performed, a gathering of the spirits.

Zong! #12

it

is said

has been decided

was justified

appeared impossible

is not necessary

is another ground

need not be proved

it

was a throwing overboard

it

is a particular circumstance

need not be proved

is another ground

is not necessary

appeared impossible

The word repeated, the word inflected, the word sung, the word chanted, the word shouted…

Remaking of words.

Remaking of the meaning of words.

What is water when it is written like this:

Zong! #1

w w w w a wa

w a w a t

er wa s

our wa

When it is sung, wailed, breathed, panted, chanted, by a room filled with celebrants bearing witness to this massacre? What happens to *this water* when it is danced?

This use of sound expands the meaning of words by creating different images behind them. The chorus and the word.

The voices and the word.

The word becomes different through the voices.

The word becomes multiple through the chorus.

The title of the work already speaks to the importance of the voice. It immediately places poetry beyond the written word by staging a reverberation: *Zong!* It is the voice – first and foremost *the voice*, not the grammar of language – that exhumes this event, that holds it aloft.

Each page of the poem's first section, 'Os', includes names of the dead at the very bottom of the page, an invocation of the dead:

to the fellow in

negro

the sustenance

in want

Rufaro Uwimana Nasiche Nafuna Asura

The need for the presence of the dead alongside the living also underscores the centrality of African ontologies of time and community to philip's work. Placing the names of the victims of *The Zong* at the bottom of each page is also a gesture to the libation, a first act in the invocation of spirits. This, again, is "i-mage" at work: the poet is evoking ancestral practices and traditions of the community. Her work relies on a sense of recognition, since the community understands the conventions at play. This submerged position is also the sea, the bottom of the ocean.

This, then, is a form of poetry that insists on the essential ties between language and body. philip's poetry, while staging the disappearance of bodies, is concerned with the ways in which language keeps bodies *disappeared*, not just in literature, but in history, and the law. But through some spirit in language itself, the poet can summon the body: these persons are physically dead, but remain present, and demand that certain duties be paid to them.

The poem becomes the occasion of a ritual in which the body's "i-mages" (its sound, its rooted ancestral memories) can reassert themselves against the dominating power of writing (law, history, Western philosophical canon, etc). In which the body can be embodied once again. Through the physicality of performance the body reclaims its rights as body. Here, poetry is inseparable from performance.

It is performance that introduces tremendous changes within the language. It is performance that restores, within the language of erasure, the "essential humanity" of a people, insofar as this can be conveyed in a collective *sound*: "The challenge is to re-create the images behind these words so that the words are being used newly." It is the body and its energies that are solicited by this visual presentation of exploded words and letters, by the multiplication of empty space. The Black body must, unfortunately, remember this trauma – the inability to understand the event, to find meaning, to make sense:

trod the grou   nd of tro
y a king in rom   e too he stro
de we hunt fo   wl at the for
t eat sip beer   from gourd s farts
and other sounds   from mouth
and ass boast s
of gold and guineas ten   guinea negroes for
one sapphire for   you rose *j ai*
faim for ruth for t   ruth
ius is just
us   the yams were
bad they sail
on a red tide o   n a die
t of bad y   am and s
our water so   me fish co
me be me   for one day *lève*
lève rise *te*   *k mi ju*
ju hold it sa   *fe for i* i
t is *ius*   & just *how i m*
iss the ci
ty the s   he negro ent
ices me wit
h her scent traps   my lust my ho   pe for you
can a b   at how about a ra
t the scen
t of you ru   th wafts acros
s oceans *dans ma c*   *hambre le code*
noir my lad
y noir e how i pet h   er *ifá i*
fa ifá the r   am tie i
t to the ma   st *le san*   *g le sang*
they sang i   sang of grace he   longs for gra
ce were w   e *ewe lu*   *a* or *fon* could
we come be m   e this my bo   d y my *sa*
ng my bon   e a rose bu   sh in the gar
den a sun r   ose in my ed
n *iye i*   *ye iye* the rose is now
sere *dis my ju*   *ju* you no
tek me *o*   *bi* round go
urds *gate* fo   *ju ju and ob*   *i* they fart p

philip's use of ritual places her in a lineage that includes Kamau Brathwaite, Aimé Césaire, Erna Brodber, and Walcott the theatre-maker. It also calls to mind contemporary performance artists in the diaspora, including Khadijah Ibrahiim, d'bi.young antiafrika and Adam Pascall.

Ritual poetry functions in freefalls. One must release the spirits in language to reveal things, to allow things to come to the surface.

...

In early December 2020, I connected to the "durational reading" which philip presents yearly, and in which she brings together a number of poets and friends to participate in what she calls a "polyvocular" performance.

It had been, of course, a particularly charged year. The conditions of the pandemic created circumstances which made it more difficult for White audiences to deny the extreme violence and systemic racism faced by Black people globally. If *Zong!* was always charged with the immediate resonance of the contemporary moment, events of the summer of 2020 made those connections even clearer. In the eyes of philip herself, the murder of George Floyd has provided new impetus to perform this ceremony.

In the performance, a pre-recorded soundtrack is overlaid by the live voices of the participants, resulting in a reverberation of voices and echoes. This pre-recorded audio guides changes and transitions. On Zoom, it is harder to sync the voices the way one would in a live gathering. In previous iterations of this durational reading – live performances – the voices were often accompanied by music from various instruments. Often, dancers share the space with the speaking, singing, or chanting performers.

Nevertheless, this presentation of *Zong!* via Zoom still manages to show its polyvocular, polyrythmic quality, in that there is a multi-layering of sounds and voices. I recalled the prayer meetings in the Church of God in my hometown of Porus, Jamaica. I recall different times and see, in my mind's eye, different moments, but one of them is days of fasting when believers cry out in tears. They voice their cares, they formulate their earnest demands. They cry out saying, "I depend on you. Whom have I to turn to but you?" There is this sweet and harmonious dissonance of voices, of crying, chanting, panting, breathing, wailing, whining, whispering, shouting. Clapping. The voice is drawn, a drawl, turning into a wail and then a moan. Then to hot tears. Then there's a plaintive song arising in a far corner of the room. And these oceanic tides keep on forming and coming until there's a crying out, a praying out, and then there is a collective stillness commanded by the knowing that we have been heard.

Then we rise.

When the air is cleansed there is a crispness, a lightness.

A hush.

A realisation of the holy moment.

This is what *Zong!* is. A cleansing.

The soundscape of a mourning.

A ceremony.

A ritual of affirmation of Black bodies. A ritual of reclamation.

GODS AND WEAPONS

Rowan Ricardo Phillips, Living Weapon, *Faber, £10.99,*
ISBN 9780571366279
Valzhyna Mort, Music for the Dead and Resurrected, *FSG, $25,*
ISBN 9780374252069

Karen McCarthy Woolf on war cries, collective memory and transformation

. . .

Brecht was not wrong. We are living in dark times and there has been singing. That singing concerns the dark times, and in this case comes from the US, via Valzhyna Mort and Rowan Ricardo Phillips, both virtuoso lyric poets operating at the top of their game.

Rowan Ricardo Phillips' *Living Weapon* is a book that is both timeless and absolutely of its time. Subtle yet explicit, supple in its range of registers and fields of enquiry, it is full of moments of alluring and sensuous detail, where the speaker waits on 'History' with "one eye half-open, like the flesh / In a shell sensing a swimmer pass –".

The collection's title refers us to the ongoing violence the black body has endured at the hands of whiteness throughout modernity, with poems such as 'Screens', a taut six-line elegy for George Floyd which concludes the volume, spotlighting a frustration at a politics where there is "no beginning or end", just a face, "slightly out of focus" floating in flames.

This public piece is a perfectly calibrated counterweight to the opening poem, 'Prelude', a deeply personal elegy, which mourns the loss of the author's grandmother, who "saw it coming and left". "It" in this case being Covid-19 and the advent of an era in which "We are all in prison. / This is the brutal lesson of the twenty-first century" ('Violins').

Music is the visible, invisible, audible and silent thread that runs through a book whose presiding spirits are lofty: "What calms you when shit hits the fan? Me? I start to hum some Beethoven, *Heiliger Dankgesang*" ('1776'). Or we might bump into Orpheus in a taxi or "[w]ade through raspberry death" to find Prince in 'Purple Elegy'. Its aspirations and its reach are at times vertiginous, taking the reader to altitudes where the air gets thin yet the atmosphere is thick with the weft of metaphysical enquiry, as in 'Who Is Less Than A Vapor?', after Donne's 'Meditation XII'. If Phillips has one unshakeable affiliation it is to pursue the dialectic, to query the association between music and poetry, to interrogate the lyric, declare it unfit for purpose and then to simultaneously reconstruct a landscape where poems that the speaker claims only "pretend to sing" sing their little hearts out – making "Music for when the music is over" ('The Peacock').

The extended opening lyric piece, a mode in which Phillips, a long-form essayist of note, excels, spans the first six pages of the book. Embedded within it is an allusion where the titular '1776' refers not only to the number of "feet in the air" at which the poem takes place, but also to a historical chronology. This includes the Declaration of Independence, which was adopted in that year, and Toni Morrison's *A Mercy* (2008), a novel set prior to that definitive historical moment, which re-envisages America before its identity as a nation state became so firmly shackled to absurd ideologies of race.

Thus the stage is set for a poetic drama in which nothing is quite as it seems. In a book liberally populated by odes, elegies and sonnets, all such musical and potentially romantic forms, 'Love Song' explodes our expectations to take American patriotism to task:

> You say love, say you're filled with love;
> Even to the edge of doom and all that.
> But how perverse and proximal hate can be,
> Like a volcano emptying itself
> Onto the small town sprouting in its shade;
> Hate ruling your continent, hate burning

Your air, hate sitting beside you under
A perfect moon, leaning in like love would

The impact of the turn is stealthy and shocking, without ever resorting to shock tactics. It is an epiphany Phillips reiterates in 'Dark Matter Ode', where, for the black father gazing wondrously at his own child sleeping, the lullaby must morph into a war cry in a world where "you asleep in your crib were a god / In the machine and that poem your father / Wrote you was a fucking living weapon".

Valzhyna Mort's *Music for the Dead and Resurrected* is powered by an equally incendiary energy. It is a book of intense necessity, written to and for the people of Belarus, the country in which Mort was born and raised before emigrating to the US; a people whose history and geography is fatally intertwined with the brutalities of Soviet imperialism. Declarative and uncompromising in its commitment to poetry's innate capacity for transformation, it is a work of startling rage and empathy, of scrutiny and protest. But before the wounds inflicted on the populace by successive dictators from Stalin to Alexander Lukashenko can begin to heal, there is collective memory to be restored, there is grandmother lore to witness and there is blood: "pig's blood / on the snow", snow that "glints and softens / a pig's slaughter" ('New Year in Vishnyowka (a lullaby)').

"Do you know what a ghost looks like?" she asks in 'Rose Pandemic'. Answer: "It looks like blood." Or, in 'Self Portrait with Madonna on Pravda Avenue', the street in Minsk on which Mort grew up and which literally, and paradoxically given its location, translates as "Truth Avenue": "A shot of snow into the blood-thick dark, / swings become guillotines, / the city of iron and irony."

Images of red and white are a motif that runs throughout the book. This is no coincidence as these are the colours of dissent worn in the mass demonstrations that swept the country in the wake of 2020's contested "re-election" of a leader who has been in power since 1994. Elsewhere, music fulfils a similar emblematic purpose as an artform of resistance, and as the title suggests, its presence is unequivocal and profound.

The accordion is the instrument on which many of the songs play out – on the streets and on the page – and here the poet manages to articulate what trauma has so often silenced. In 'Ode to Branca', one of several poems in the book that reference the impact of Chernobyl on the human and non-human environment (see also 'Nocturne for a Moving Train' and 'Music for Girls' Voice and Bison'), the personification of the landscape recalls its devastating effects with characteristic and chilling brevity: "If the sun appears inside its boneless sky," Mort writes, "the sky is diagnosed with a tumor." But in music, there remains some redemption, even in a country where propaganda, misinformation and ubiquitous state violence has long been rife: "What has kept us alive? Our death songs. // How did we scare God / Out of this place?"

God's absence is echoed in 'Psalm 18'. When the speaker prays to the trees she finds that "language migrates down my legs like mute cattle". Mort has Belarusian, Russian and English at her disposal, and while the poems are written in English, their poetics operate under a different star, where the limitations of any language based only on words are transcended. She also deploys synaesthetic metaphor to powerful effect: "If there'd be a sound between us, / let it be one that starts / with touch, / which is music" ('Rose Pandemic').

Family and what we stand to inherit and pass on between generations are preoccupations in both of these collections. In Mort's opening poem, 'To Antigone, A Dispatch', the speaker makes an offer, in terms that are hard to resist, to Sophocles' heroine (who is denied by her own sister) to be the sibling she never had. Together they will the clean the house "the way only two sisters can", there will be "no bones scattered like dirty socks, / no ashes at the bottom of kneecaps". What her homeland has attempted to cover up, she will unearth: "Under the moth-eaten snow / my motherland has good bones."

She writes with meticulous affection of a grandmother whose stories are both personal and iconic to the history of Belarus, stories that respond to the temperature of their time and surroundings like mercury in a thermometer ('Baba Bronya'). Women's stories that have been uttered then shushed, in the name of safety and survival. Stories that speak of 'An Attempt at Geneaology' and, via a communal history, of 'Genesis':

Under Criminal Record
Write, "Mother, home."
Under Weapon
Write, "Mother, home."

Karen McCarthy Woolf was a Fulbright Scholar and Poet-in-Residence at the Promise Institute for Human Rights at UCLA in 2019–20.

COMIC MASK, TRAGIC MASK

Christopher Reid, The Late Sun, *Faber, £14.99,*
ISBN 9780571360246
Heidi Williamson, Return by Minor Road, *Bloodaxe, £9.95,*
ISBN 9781780375229

John Greening on playfulness, seriousness and risk

...

Many readers will know Christopher Reid from his 2009 Costa-winning elegies, *A Scattering*, but he has always been more in thrall to the comic muse, from his early examples of Martian wit gathered in the *Penguin Book of Contemporary British Poetry* (1982) to the delightful two-hander, *The Song of Lunch* (2009), which was made into a surprisingly effective television drama. There are not many other poets who would have as the opening line to their latest collection "Less limber than a lemur" – although in fact the ludic chords of 'Arboristics' come after a preliminary poem, 'Photography', which establishes a more meditative key: "With the time an hour to lunch / the restaurant door stands open". We could almost be back with Emma Thompson and Alan Rickman in the TV play. But in this scene there are no characters, just tables "poised, / Laundered and starched" and "All human fuss is backstage" while the poet's attention (he is artist as much as dramatist) is on "a cool, square depth / of shadow and nuance, / fixed for an instant, an age." That nonlemur, incidentally, turns out to be a tree surgeon, and 'Arboristics' a poem that Marianne Moore would have seen a reason for.

Reid loves the monkey business of poetry, of life indeed, and has the gift of relishing and revivifying the ordinary, whether it's girls giggling, children running at the sea, a dog by the side of the road (he published a whole collection of dog poems), an empty bookshop, a suburban magnolia, or a sunset. The title poem takes hold of the cliché and dusts it down, describing the sun as if it were a recently deceased cinematographer ("His work was highly regarded / in the business [...] His art was both / panoramic and minutely detailed.") in a manner reminiscent of Dennis O'Driscoll. There are many examples of such playfulness, which left this reviewer wishing he had thought of them first – 'Smells of London', for instance, and 'Prose', which begins:

> Prose pays a call on poetry.
> A seafaring tower block,
> palatial, proud, pristinely white
> as if fresh from the drawing board
> of some high-minded architect,
> has arrived to inspect
> the tired old city.
> It comes as a shock

In a similar vein, 'Ink' is a kind of comic take on Heaney's 'From the Land of...' allegories (Reid is currently editing Heaney's letters). 'Encounters with Local Spirits and Gods' is an entertaining short sequence dedicated to contemporary deities – the Goddess of Shopping, the God of Grilled Fish. We are in fact constantly entertained, and some of the work is indisputably light verse (Auden would have approved) but Reid makes room for serious subjects, usually with a positive spin: tributes to 'Malala' (Yousafzai – "she spoke up / and won't shut up"), to his barber, Mustafa, "a victim of the virus" ('Death of a Barber'), and to a 103-year-old composer. I only wish 'In Memoriam Elliott Carter' had been available for a music anthology I edited – true also of 'Le Tombeau de Ravel', a villanelle which boldly rhymes 'Bolero' with two words more usually associated with Disney's *Hercules*.

Reid can be warmly human, as in the poems about his parents or the simple facts of 'Unheard Words', addressing a stroke victim, the quietly concealed internal rhymes (which run throughout the poem) reinforcing the idea of a cruel game as attempts to communicate founder:

> At each failed go, a modest smile of baffled
> endeavour, as if this game could be played forever.
> It could not, though. The last morning I called,
> all words, all thoughts, were hushed, as, turned towards
> the wall, you slept. I whispered my farewell.

But there is latent anger and bitterness in the subversively titled refugee poem, 'A Cold Going', and in 'War Song for Civilians', whose obsessive rhymes alone give an idea of the poem's trajectory: *trust / dust / rust / lust / just / gust / crust / concussed / dust*. Reid is an excellent and fearless satirist (think of his glorious romp, *Six Bad Poets*), mocking "enormous male babies" he notes on the streets "in comical baseball cap, / shapeless T-shirt / and huge, flapping shorts" ('Boomers'). Even his poem about the "ghost" bicycles that litter London streets has a sardonic edge: "Oh, get over it, it's the vernacular now; and what's not to like / about 'Out with the whited sepulchre! In with the whited bike'?" ('White Bicycles'). There is formal ingenuity even in the most apparently straightforward of pieces here, and part of the pleasure comes from the interaction of form and subject – which, it should hardly need saying, is what poetry is all about. If I had to recommend a collection as treatment for lockdown blues, *The Late Sun* might well be it.

Heidi Williamson came to prominence with her striking second collection, *The Print Museum* (2016), which used the vocabulary and methods of typography with a playful relish that Christopher Reid would surely appreciate. Her new book is different, but again has a theme, although not one to ease any anxieties. At the heart of *Return by Minor Road* is the massacre at a primary school in Dunblane, which occurred when Williamson was living in that community in 1996. Every poet has a story that they know might one day become a book (an epigraph quotes Eimear McBride: "The things I do not want to write about become the things I write about"), but there are considerable risks involved in the Dunblane story – questions of tone and tact become crucial. The opening section ('What the river leaves behind') only hints at the tragedy, setting the poet's own domestic life next to memories of Scotland and especially the rivers and lochs. Occasionally the two converge, as in 'Thrawn':

In sleep, my eyelids fail to close
completely. Two small moons
shiver below unsettled lashes.

It's then I go back to the river.

Not all the poems feel fully achieved – is all that repetition of "out" and "on" in 'Weir' a deliberate effect? – but the sense of something brewing is well sustained. In 'Cormorant', the "*Run-hide-fight* [...] active shooter drill" taught to American schoolchildren is transferred to the bird of the title, which in turn represents the poet's own conflicted feelings. There is considerable formal variety in this section (allegory in 'Loch Occasional', a prose poem, and an apt 'erasure' of her own early 'Woodcutter') and the last few poems are especially potent: 'Fugitive dust' is literally haunting, and there is a lovely group of three poems featuring hares.

The book's central section, 'Cold Spring: 13 March 1996', is in effect a sequence about the shooting. Perhaps no poet could be equal to such a tragedy, but Williamson does what she can, chiefly (and wisely) by presenting us with aspects of what she herself apparently experienced, using shock juxtaposition in the first two poems, then deliberately banal narrative ("The last time I saw you, / really saw you, was in the office / that day when the announcements / started to come, but no one / understood yet what had happened") and later elegiac anaphora, including the bare list of victims' names. The experimental use of space deployed so brilliantly in 'The Case' (Williamson's witty sequence in *The Print Museum*) is here given serious work to do, the lacunae of 'Cold Spring' expressing how everyone is lost for words. This puts enormous pressure on the words that remain, but by and large Williamson achieves the necessary Arvo Pärt-like intensity as the section moves (shifting at the same time from "I to "We") towards the consolations of nature.

Her third section completes an arc, with poems about everyday life in the aftermath, and how trauma breaks into it. Indeed, a poem called 'Every day' describes escorting a child "all the way to his classroom door / [...] I text you to say we arrived safely. / I text you to say I collected him", and how when the speaker sees an ambulance, she panics. But there is healing too, the river, the forest. The collection's title poem appears here, an account of revisiting Dunblane (too understated, perhaps, and wouldn't "Dark pillars of fir" sound better than "firs"?) grouped with several others about the area, formally diverse as ever. *Return by Minor Road* (an excellent title) is admirably constructed, and while the whole makes a greater impression than the parts, it is a book Heidi Williamson was destined to write.

> *John Greening's recent books include* The Silence *(Carcanet, 2019) and* Vapour Trails: Reviews and Essays on Poetry *(Shoestring, 2020).*

A LONG TIME DEAD

Shane McCrae, Sometimes I Never Suffered, *Corsair, £10.99,*
ISBN 9781472155801
J.O. Morgan, The Martian's Regress, *Cape, £10,*
ISBN 9781787332140

Kit Fan on angels and aliens

. . .

Emerging from the rich tapestry of angels and heaven woven by the hands of Dante, Milton, Blake and Rilke, Shane McCrae's *Sometimes I Never Suffered* is a daringly original reimagination of heaven which engages with history, politics, race, and memory. The book concludes a stunning trilogy, preceded by *In the Language of My Captor* (2017), which portrays a fast-paced purgatory of racial complicity and redemption, and *The Gilded Auction Block* (2019), a filmic reconfiguration of our contemporary hell. It's rare to discover a poet who masters the alchemy of form and music, vision and structure with such surgical control and improvisatory freedom. Every word, line and gap in lieu of punctuation gets under the reader's skin, as if McCrae has ingested the ghosts of Whitman, Eliot, Ginsberg and Beckett to compose a mesmerising rhapsody about the master and the slave, the unjust and the remembered, the lonely and the divine.

Sometimes I Never Suffered opens with Jim Limber, the biracial adopted son of Jefferson Davis, speaking from heaven in a voice that remembers the language of Genesis, Lewis Carroll's nonsensical logic, and Beckett's late prose: "I've been a long time dead without my life / And when it comes back it comes back to me / In parts" ('Jim Limber in Heaven Is a Nexus at Which the Many Heavens of the Multiverse Converge'). Holding ten syllables, the lines create an uncanny momentum with unpredictable breathing gaps and verbal repetitions that juggle comedy, confusion, and poignancy within the space of fourteen lines. Syllabics and sonnets (and their many mutated forms) are McCrae's bow and strings throughout the book, as he acrobatically adopts, refurnishes, or abandons rhymes like Emily Dickinson and Paul Muldoon. Apart from the historical Jim Limber, another key protagonist is "the hastily assembled angel", who considers their own angelic existence alongside a variety of human experiences including care, love, vitality, freedom, loneliness, the lives of dogs and people. In McCrae's hand, the angel embodies a vulnerability and inquisitiveness that mirror Jim Limber's own. Since Jacob, many have wrestled with the angel, but few have managed to capture the existential predicament between the human and the divine, as McCrae does in 'The Hastily Assembled Angel Meets the God of Human Freedom', in which the angel watches as "the guards waved their empty hands / To say *There is no food in the city*" and "The humans in their freedom made a giant calf with / A golden body". Like a blood transfusion, the Old Testament travels back to the future, prompting us to rethink the causes of idolatry, famine, poverty, imagination and freedom.

The shimmering soul of the book is revealed most clearly in the two-part 'Variations on Jim Limber Goes to Heaven', consisting of twenty-one sonnets (bar one poem which is a moving dialogue between Limber and Davis) as eclectic and virtuosic as Beethoven's Diabelli Variations. Each poem takes on an ambitious topic such as 'Truth About His Fate', 'Ever-Growing Hunger for the New', 'Jesus and the Mongrel Dog', but drills down to the nitty-gritty of inequality and brutality, for example, in the concluding lines of 'Jim Limber on White Embrace', where a sense of belonging is injured by the painful realisation that "Heaven   ain't plenty and it ain't protection / Heaven is when they kill you in their homes". The most memorable of McCrae's variations is 'Jim Limber Tells What He Knows About Heaven' which reads like an impossible blend of hymn, tongue-twister, Miles Davis blues improvisation, short Spike Lee film, and song stolen from Huck Finn:

Heaven's a horse a train a ship with no
Captain or with a captain but the captain is
A Negro   or a rowboat tied but loose-
ly to   the dock the river peaceful no-
body or everybody is   a Ne-
gro it's a hundred Negroes on the dock
A thousand Negros like when Jesus broke
The bread to feed ten   thousand peo-
ple maybe fifteen and the bread just grew
And grew the dock just grows and grows beneath them
Ten thousand Negros cheering you to freedom
A hundred thousand and you got good shoes
And walk to the rowboat smiling and untie it
But Heaven ain't you running but you staying

Reading it out loud twenty times, it feels as if the sonnet (the poem and form) has been gifted the "good shoes" it needs to walk through centuries of social history about black and white, land and exploration, peace and struggle, bread and miracle. Like the sonnet, this is a book that runs and stays, and should be reread every year, if not every season or month.

If McCrae's book is like a symphony, Morgan's *The Martian's Regress* is like a sci-fi remake fuelled by elaborate description and sensory overload. It retells an apocalyptic story of a post-disaster world constructed out of that genre's familiar terrain, in the vein of the Martian School associated with Craig Raine and Christopher Reid in 1970s and '80s. Stanley Kubrick observes that "the destruction of this planet would have no significance on a cosmic scale", and familiarity is the soul of the sci-fi genre, which depends on the motifs of isolation, nostalgia, discovery and return. On the one hand, *The Martian's Regress* is a compelling satire of human endeavour and survival, a devastating cautionary tale of what could happen to our planet if "There's no price for progress" ('Frequently Asked Questions')". On the other hand, it's weighed down by the deadpan urgency of a distant, third-person speaker obsessed with describing every action, decision, and predicament of the Martian in relentless detail, giving the poems the air of being trapped by "a cumbersome religiosity" ('The Martian Visits the Museum'). Morgan is a seasoned storyteller, and his mercurial imagination is evident throughout, but the poems are so jam-packed with explanations that they leave little room for surprise or imaginative possibility. It's sometimes as if the winged sandals of Mercury, god of eloquence and guide to the underworld, have lost their potency. At times the poems seem to stare at the reader dispassionately out of the void, but a void that, like the condition Morgan describes in 'Desecrations', is "overcomplicated".

If "Death is the mother of beauty", as Wallace Stevens proposed, the apocalypse is in many ways the father of poetry. From the Book of Revelation to Milton's *Paradise Lost*, Eliot's *The Waste Land* to Gunn's *Misanthropos*, poetry has witnessed various forms of destruction, actual or fictional, and many apocalyptic poems balance chance and inevitability, hope and despair, redemption and damnation, the rational and the absurd. *The Martian's Regress* is no exception. Morgan's episodic documentary catalogues the Martian's life in elaborate detail, including his 'Ancestral Tales', his android female companion ("A womanly shell with the woman removed"), how he toasts bread in 'Martian Toasting Ritual', how he commutes, hunts, makes love, visits the museum, desecrates a cathedral, cooks last suppers, etc. In poem after poem, the speaker visualises and destabilises our familiar life by repeating loss and loneliness through the Martian's desensitised existence, reconnecting the force of elegy through the refusal to elegise. It feels like the uncanny has been robbed by a diligent muse working with "dispassionate logical scrutiny", pushing the poems over the edge as a form of experiment. Craig Raine's Martian postcard has acquired epic proportions.

"Every new work is in some way a departure", Morgan has said in an interview, and his experimental flair is evident throughout *The Martian's Regress* which uses form, pattern, and meter kaleidoscopically, what he calls "polymetrics, or mixed measure". Despite its formal assurances and ambitious agenda, the book reads like an unresolved experiment, for example, in the final poem 'Soul, Searching':

> How can you tell if this is a soul half-full
>   or a soul half-empty?
> It depends upon what was poured into the soul
> and why it was so unfulfilling
> or upon who attempted to drain it and why they too
> so soon gave up.

These lines echo Rilke's searching and haunting angelism, and yet foster a furious Morganian hollowness, captured in the throttled rhyme of "the soul" with both "half-full" and "unfulfilling". *The Martian's Regress* is dedicated to "a companionable soul", an ambition at odds with the soulless companionship the book projects, with its bleak vision of the earth of lost voices and cancelled reverberations. The book is a dark variant of a familiar dystopia, as in 'The Natural Course of Things', where the speaker observes "All this had been foreseen, such cycles are predictable".

> *Kit Fan's latest poetry collection is* As Slow As Possible *(Arc, 2018). His debut novel* Diamond Hill *is forthcoming from Dialogue Books in May.*

THE GREEN FUSE

Apocalypse: An Anthology, *ed. James Keery, Carcanet, £19.99,*
ISBN 9781784108182

Chris Moss on the endurance of apocalypse

...

In 1940 R.A. Caton's Fortune Press – equally famous for publishing Dylan Thomas's *18 Poems* and works of gay erotica, and for not respecting copyright – published a collection of poetry with the title *The New Apocalypse*. The volume's editors were the poets J.F. Hendry and Henry Treece, who included their own verses alongside those of Norman MacCaig, Robert Melville and Dylan Thomas. The book was a success, and Hendry and Treece issued two further anthologies of poetry and prose with apocalyptic titles: *The White Horseman* (Routledge, 1941) and *The Crown and the Sickle* (King & Staples, 1945).

Carcanet's *Apocalypse*, writes editor James Keery, aims to "take a fresh look" at the theme and period, "on the initially disorientating premise that the central body of work is Dylan Thomas". The 1933 publication of the then teenage Thomas's 'The force that through the green fuse' was, the anthology contends, as important a moment as T.S. Eliot's *The Waste Land* or Yeats's 'The Second Coming', inspiring a neglected strain of neo-romantic poetry that deserves more attention.

Containing 330 poems by more than 200 poets (including works by all 21 authors included in the original three anthologies), *Apocalypse* is not the testimony of a poetic school; no manifesto, locale or publisher links authors as varied as George Barker, W.S. Graham, Edith Sitwell and Rosemary Tonks. But the poems in *Apocalypse*, arranged in the order of poets' birth dates, are informed and unified by a number of traditions and events. A presiding theme, especially in poems written by those who lived through them as adults, are the two world wars – particularly the 1939–45 war, with its bombers, razed cities and searchlights. The lexicon of a common Christian biblical heritage surfaces in many poems, rubbing against new languages emanating from technology, mass communications, political unrest and class division, as well as the artistic convulsions of Modernism, Cubism and Surrealism.

Edward Thompson's 'In Patmos: I' (1942) splices aviatorial visions with the thoughts of St John in exile on the Greek island:

> I John saw these things:
> I saw Lucifer fall
> Shot down in flames,
> Clawed down, his wings
> Cleft by a boy

Thompson's John is writing "when the seas / Were a fire, when the mind was afire". The external world mirrors the internal one. Icarus has been replaced by Satan and every pilot is as violent as the devil himself, even if he too is doomed to crash and burn.

The New Testament's Book of Revelation is full of fire, brimstone, thunderclaps and coded images of seals, stars and horses. As every conscientious RE pupil will remember, "apocalypse" is a Greek word meaning "to uncover" – a notion most lucidly expressed in Matthew's Gospel 27:51: "Then, behold, the veil of the temple was torn in two from top to bottom; and the earth quaked, and the rocks were split." Richness of imagery, sometimes verging on Blakeian hallucination, and seeing, or writing, through this to discover some other, deeper reality are guiding principles for many apocalyptic-minded authors.

In her powerful poem 'Four Men's Desire' (1949), Sheila Wingfield, whose husband Mervyn suffered shell shock during the Second World War, also addresses John of Patmos, as well as John the Baptist, the apostle John and St John the evangelist. She considers whether the "barbarous

Apocalypse" of Revelation comprises the "Great visions of a lunatic / Or a world convulsed and sick", concluding that the humane, hope-giving desires of the four Johns persist, buried beneath the charred remains of civilisation. The poem's clinching assertion that "Earth knows four men's desire" suggests love is stored as a kind of metaphysical lava while allowing a pantheistic image of the planet as a living mind. A lot of apocalyptic writing embraces this kind of eco-theology.

That reality might be rent apart – and some deep truth brought to light – by the exercise of thought and language has obvious appeal to poets. But there are a number of ways one might achieve the state that permits such a vision. Robert Graves appeals to "Lady Morphia" to vanquish pain and terror. Blanaid Salkeld employs a Dada-like, anarchic verse form, her syntax full of gaps and dead ends. Hugh MacDiarmid gets his visions from a Chambers dictionary, his "found" poems spilling over with obscure coinages.

What Dylan Thomas does, in 'The force that through the green fuse', is combine elements of all these, allying youthful lyricism to garish, apocalyptic imagery, to discover – or, indeed, force – a new consciousness:

> The lips of time leech to the fountain head;
> Love drips and gathers, but the fallen blood
> Shall calm her sores.
> And I am dumb to tell a weather's wind
> How time has ticked a heaven round the stars

Thomas's galloping metre freights an energy so violently vital that it can become its opposite: the "green fuse" that "drives my green age" bends youth with a "wintry fever". Life and death, youth and age, creation and annihilation, are looped in a vortex. The poem is perforation and transmission ("drives", "streams", "spring", "sucks", "whirl", "stirs", "leech", "drips"). Time, nature and the body pulsate and, pierced, pour forth an ebbing life. Thomas's "green fuse" is a searingly beautiful abstraction that links Wordsworth with Max Ernst's *Europe after the Rain II*, Freud with St Francis of Assisi, Wilfred Owen with Ted Hughes. The poet's ego and body, merged with nature, are where the twentieth-century apocalypse unfolds.

In 'The Poet' (1939), Lawrence Durrell, who went pub-crawling with Dylan Thomas – and shared his interest in Surrealism – also makes the narrator the central object of his psychodrama and recasts St John-like symbolism as pagan cosmogony: "Nine moons heard of my coming / The drumming of mythical horses / On the walls of the womb." Laurie Lee does something similar in 'Thistle' (1946) and 'The Edge of Day' (1951), though with nature as the prompt – pricking skin and filling the beholder's eye with "a chaos [...] Where molten worlds are born".

J.F. Hendry's 'Apocalypse' is printed on the page opposite his 'Picasso – for Guernica' (both 1940; the Fortune Press anthology featured a Picasso drawing on the frontispiece). In the poems he piles up images of wounds, bones, blood and a "cannibal sky" that read like the verses of the Book of Revelation filtered directly through the Second World War. Across the anthology, one senses how poets were struggling to devise a grammar suited to the latest horrors; where plastic artists could make bodies collapse and spatial dimensions crumble on their canvases, and twelve-tone musicians could resort to unmelodious structures and near-cacophony, poets needed to find a way to communicate a magnitude of horror and a degree of disorder that demanded more than the traditional tools of dissonance, caesura, half-rhyme and such. "Neigh, horse, terror through steel teeth and a thicket / Of bricks!", writes Hendry; verbs just won't cut it anymore. The Picasso poem ends ranting and raving: "I am the eyeball blown world! Axis of anger!"

In far mellower tones, R.S. Thomas, in 'Maes-yr-Onnen' (1948) laments the fact that a poet, for all that he describes a chapel "stone by stone", "painting faithfully the mossed tiles and the tree", cannot in truth draw the hearer/reader close to his intimate experience. For Thomas, any vision is a private affair; he would go on to become the priest-poet of the eschatological mode. The Welsh would seem to have a penchant for apocalyptic thinking – no fewer than 16 poets contained here are born or resident in, or otherwise associated with, Wales. In 'Poem from Llanybri' (1941), underrated poet Lynette Roberts seems to offer respite from the mad whirl of modernity, inviting the reader to "sit by the hearth with blue flames rising", twice alluding to "the old way": a simpler way of living and being. But the prose poem, 'The New Perception of Colour' (1941), turns the Luftwaffe's bombing of Swansea into a aesthetic-chemical event: "Oh! look how lovely she looks caught in those lights! Oh!" The satire is of art as much as war. Again, "blue flames rising" in her cottage seem to provide a narrow sort of solace.

If the connections between the poems seem loose, even tenuous at times, then that's because the temple of the New Apocalytics is a very broad church. For Keery, the tradition can also be termed "visionary modernism", a counter to "familiar ironic modernism, epitomised by W.H. Auden". But there was nothing fringe about this movement, even if later criticism has tended to prefer the ironic, urbane mode and those authors who, like Eliot, sought to position poetry as one branch of a wider intellectual movement. 'Little Gidding' could well have been included here, alongside Yeats's later verse, as well as poems by the likes of Edwin Muir and Stevie Smith. But as Keery notes, "their celebrity will hardly be missed. I have been after the best, but have opted, other things being equal, for the less familiar".

It was a wise decision. The sheer range of voices on display in *Apocalypse: An Anthology* is as thrilling as the poems are at times challenging, even difficult (in the way a Bartók piano concerto is difficult). Social realism, naturalism and academic intellectualism routinely win out in British writing, and the canon has suppressed the riskier, more idiolectal strain in literature. Apocalyptic poetry was largely derided from the 1950s and to be called a "New Romantic", even today, is to be marginalised from the mainstream. But a society hides its apocalyptic intimations at its peril. "It might never happen," say the dystopians. "It already has," declare the apocalyptics – but there is hope beyond the fire, new life in the ashes.

Chris Moss is the author of a cultural history of Patagonia and a literary compendium for London commuters.

THE OTHER SIDE

Glyn Maxwell, How the Hell Are You, *Picador, £10.99,*
ISBN 9781529037739
Alan Gillis, The Readiness, *Picador, £10.99,*
ISBN 9781529037661

Ben Wilkinson on poetic voice, formal prowess, and strange times

. . .

Paul Farley took the pulse at the turn of our millennium when he quipped that contemporary poets haven't had criticism, they've had marketing. In an age where marketing's role in matters aesthetic is ever-increasing, the individual voice can be an overvalued commodity, playing to a perceived appetite for poet-as-author. It is refreshing, then, to encounter Glyn Maxwell's *How the Hell Are You*, a collection of poems whose unfashionably complex play with poetic voice recognises and exploits the ultimate impersonality of writing – how it is only ever language that speaks, acts, and performs. But then Maxwell has always done his own thing, ever since he set the empty roundabout spinning in the first poem of his first collection, some thirty years ago. Formally dextrous, syntactically inventive, able to combine authentic emotion with self-reflexive dramatisation: for those in the know, a Maxwell collection is an event. Recent books *Hide Now* (2008) and *Pluto* (2013) marked him out as both entertaining and hard-thinking, contemporary while in pursuit of timelessness, putting into practice the poetics outlined in his essay volume *On Poetry* (2012), essential reading for anyone serious about their writing craft. He simply asks more of his poems and his readers than most poets dare or are able to.

But Maxwell isn't the kind of experimentalist content to play games with language. His poems succeed for blending dramatised voices with painfully human concerns, reckoning with our times (and time itself) with a wry awareness that typically avoids archness, skewering our self-centred haplessness while remaining compassionate. Take 'Song of AI', one of a number of poems in *How the Hell Are You* that gives an assessment of our species from the perspective of artificial intelligence:

> We see the people whom you love
> hate people whom you hate. It is not lost
> on us that if you turn to that
>   we will not
> be noticed at our work. Because our work
>
> will be the same as yours.

Here, as elsewhere in the book, a kind of anonymised lyric intelligence cuts to the quick. Freed from the distracting restrictions of a particular and coherent persona, the poem unpacks our increasingly machine-like certainties in a digital age. Binary opinions are similarly satirised in 'The Other Side', as searing a portrayal of our world of Brexit, fake news, and Twitter flame wars as you will read: "The other side must hate us why would anyone / we're angels we mean well we have a battle on / if they can't see our wings all fucking hope is gone." Indeed. Under the unflinching gaze of these poems, even the places we might variously seek comfort or refuge are exposed as empty or sham. In 'Bluebirds Over', which takes lyrics from the nostalgic British wartime song popularised by Vera Lynn, the mawkish nursery-rhyme-like patter is amplified into a nightmarish litany, while 'The Heyday' simply concludes "the answer to most of my questions is *Nowhere*, / the rest *Search me*". Even the act of writing is stripped back and debunked – or rather, the clumsy ego of the writer themselves, forever obscuring the poem from telling its truth. "May I say I had a dream of / something too?" enquires the blank page of the poet sat before it. "Obviously not and off you go now." "I too feel nothing", confesses 'Sonnet at a Loss'. "I was made one day / in private joy by one who can't explain me, / reach me, or change me now." But if there is hope in the deluded and self-deceiving set of contemporary circumstances that Maxwell ingeniously presents here, it is in meaningful language and its profound effects – in great poetry and literature itself, no less. As 'Page of First Old Book He Read' reflects of a child's wondrous gaze at its markings, "three memories stay with me":

> his grin away and back again as if
> he'd found somewhere
>   we both belonged – slow turning
> I took for love – and, when time called enough,
>   light narrowing so gently.

Alan Gillis is a Northern Irish writer who deserves to be much more widely read, so it is reassuring to see his fifth collection, *The Readiness*, appear with Picador. Like Maxwell, he is an outward-looking poet and formally adept, too. His adaptive use of poetic line and speech rhythms in negotiating human struggles between inner and outer worlds often recalls MacNeice, but also Gillis's late compatriot Ciaran Carson, to whom this book is dedicated. But while there is a contemplative seriousness to these poems, there is also – almost always – exuberance. 'Blossom Drift (22nd May 2017)' might respond to the horrors of the Manchester Arena bombing, but it does so with a touchingly defiant portrait of young girls, "six, seven or eight years old", who "circle and chatter in some form / of dance or ritual in the garden":

> If there is a holy war, let heaven
> assemble a nation army of pink
> deely bobbers and purple nail glitter,
> butterfly face paint, marching to a play-
>
> list of Beyoncé, Rihanna, Ariana:
> let each follow the steps, learn the moves
> of the dance with a gleam in her face
> and unclenched fists, free from fear.

Elsewhere, the book is worth the price of entry for its rhythmically loquacious way with language, as in 'The Return':

> If you take a moment outdoors as the day
> undays itself, you might spot that swift prowler,
> that tuft-tailed razortooth, red-stealthed stealer:
> the estate's stray fox in the darkblue dusk.
>
> You might hear that thornball in the shadows:
> the hedgehog below the hedgerow –
> wee nimble-nosed needlepelt, prickleback –
> its spiny shuffle through dead leaves.

Fizzing with vernacular and bounding rhythms, yet also precisely lyrical, the poems in *The Readiness* frequently run away with themselves, attempting to keep up with, and make some sense of, the often digital babble and information overload of our age. Even getting ready of a workaday morning, the poet spots us "set for the whigmaleeries of the ticking clock, / spilt milk, the mystery / of missing socks, the transport peeve, the hundred-tonne / weight of to-dos" ('Before the Bustle of Day'). Meanwhile, the strange dreamscape of 'Metropolis' depicts a "*Titanic*-themed bar fuelled by Tinder / and frustration / where every empty glass fumed with accusation". But rather than simply glare at the world through a screen or situated perspective, Gillis is able to reflect both our private and public selves back at us, in poems that are as capacious and various as the come-and-go places they situate themselves. Take 'Flat White Afternoon', where "the guy eating flatbread" sits alone "with five thousand / friends on his phone", across from the woman "wiping / the small child's chin / delighting an on- / looker at the next / table", and "a clutch / of mitching girls / with pierced noses / and Tintin / hairdos who look / at you as if to say / is it dial-a-dickhead / day in here?"

The Readiness impresses, but more importantly moves and surprises, given Gillis's ability to combine dry humour with insight, vibrant description with direct address, and contemporary relevance with lasting concerns. "In the wink of an eye all you know drifts / away but who benefits from sorrow?" asks our poet in 'The Response'. Like its title poem, this is a collection that recognises how "under a harvest moon, / in a lift, on the stairs, / in an encrypted chatroom: / it could happen anywhere."

Ben Wilkinson's second collection, Same Difference, *is due from Seren in 2022. A reader's guide to the poetry of Don Paterson is forthcoming.*

DOUBLE CONSCIOUSNESS

Caroline Bergvall, Alisoun Sings, *Nightboat, $16.95,*
ISBN 9781643620015
James Womack, Homunculus, *Carcanet, £10.99,*
ISBN 9781784109912

Kathryn Maris on persona poems, translation and temporal leaps

...

Where did all the personae go? Andrea del Sarto, Prufrock, the seven at the Golden Shovel, the Lammas hireling, the world's wives, the mechanic who explains (very simply) topping up the brake fluid? The 1990s saw a revival of invented poetic personae; later, the device seemed to wane, perhaps for understandable reasons. Lyric directness from voices previously absent in English-language poetry was required more urgently than blank verse narrated by a duke. Anxieties about appropriation occupied literary discourse, as did dialogues about redress. When a portion of Sasha Dugdale's long poem 'Joy' – spoken by Catherine Blake, widow of William – won the Forward Prize for Best Single Poem in 2016, the use of the monologue form was admired – yes. But perhaps more admired was Dugdale's triumph in 'giving voice' to a female artist whose labours on behalf of her husband were inadequately acknowledged. The poem was recognised as a corrective.

In fact, persona poems haven't gone anywhere: they've retained their place in many contemporary collections. These, however, may not be the poems that gain public acclaim, so the device may only seem to be in decline. One common argument is that all poems are persona poems, even the most manifestly autobiographical. While that is surely true, to deny authorial intent is disingenuous. A poem that attempts to record personal experience candidly, with a so-called 'authentic' voice, is not the same as one that resorts to blatant artificiality or adopts the point of view of a fictional character. Perhaps the effect is the same, perhaps the end result is always some version of 'the poet'. But why not distinguish between a poem that foregrounds the self and another which seeks (successfully or not) to obscure it? And why not ask what each mode can achieve at its best?

Recent collections by Caroline Bergvall and James Womack are atypical – even groundbreaking – books that encourage us to entertain these questions, and more. Both authors find a Poundian intersection between translation and dramatic monologue; both make joyful use of anachronism and temporal leaps; and both rescue humourless circumstances with wit, song and forthright sexuality.

Bergvall's *Alisoun Sings* is the more explicitly political. "Alisoun" refers to the character in Chaucer's 'The Miller's Tale' who is "caughte [...] by the queynte" – a phrase that would seem to portend Donald Trump's imperative to "grab 'em by the pussy". Does Bergvall sing through Alisoun, or is Bergvall the voice through whom Alisoun sings? As the two main participants in this polyphonic work of intersectional feminism, "Alisoun" and "Caroline" are occasionally combative alter-egos. Sometimes their relationship is like a marriage, sometimes a bitter divorce. The "Caroline" character writes, "I have to concede that all the years of being bullied and harassed, bitched about, and fighting with you, Alisoun, are bringing me back to my own time [. . .] full of a fighting spirit."

Bergvall, a master of sound, language and idiolect, riffs off Chaucerian Middle English, while offering readers a helping hand through phonetic spellings and contemporary idiom. "Baby light ma fire! A thousand songs preparen a night of true lovin'". The crashing together of 'Middle English' with modes such as text speak ("Somme me found 2 sexy, and some 2 saucy"), hashtags ("#mytime #is #nou #!"), references to Twitter and "FB", and even Latin ("Odi et amo") creates a weird and startling but glorious music. Sometimes "Caroline" takes over in clear contemporary English, recording her dreams and interrogating their meaning. At other times "Caroline" writes sparky and performative versions of the lyric essay in which writers such as Kathy Acker and Sara Ahmed are not merely quoted, but turn up as characters, as though in a Platonic symposium. While most of the book is in prose, there are shouty slogan-y lists, and centos made from twentieth-century song lyrics. These are reminiscent of the exultant centos (collaged from favourite poems) in Maureen N. McLane's hybrid memoir *My Poets* (2012), which Bergvall may have read – because one gets the sense that Bergvall has read insatiably, across centuries, and retained it in photographic detail. At the end, a section called 'Bookes' contains a meticulous bibliography of authors, from Christine de Pizan to Arundhati Roy. If such layering of language, tones and approaches seems over-complicated, it isn't. Bergvall hops light-footedly from section to section, each of which moves with rapid energy.

Alisoun Sings offers a radical approach to the dramatic monologue. While preserving the basic integrity of a single voice, it fashions a communal female voice based on literature (and songs) across centuries – but with "Alisoun" and "Caroline" at its base. The resulting voice is fluid, queer, sexualised, angry, ecstatic and self-reflective. *Alisoun Sings* is also a radical approach to translation. Bergvall has practised translation throughout her career, from her improvisatory piece *VIA: 48 Dante Variations* (2000), to *Meddle English* (2011) and *Drift* (2014). The latter two works form, along with *Alisoun Sings*, a multilectical trilogy in which ancient stories (including Chaucer's, most of which were themselves derived through 'imitation' and translation) are repurposed, while language itself is interrogated, disrupted and (in the case of *Drift*) fragmented. This pioneering trilogy could not have ended more triumphantly – although "Alisoun" assures us that "the era of ma tellings nat bygone, just bigonne".

If there is a performative merging of author and persona in *Alisoun Sings*, a similar unification occurs in James Womack's *Homunculus*. The persona in this case is Maximian (or Maximianus), often identified as "the last of the Roman poets". Womack states in an afterword that, although loosely based on Maximian's elegies (which total 686 lines), his own elegiac six-part poem of 2,200 lines is not a translation. Nor does he refer to it as a version, assuming we accept a distinction between versions and translations. That Womack is a linguist and translator (from Russian and Spanish) makes one inclined to trust his assessment and not worry that Maximian's name has been omitted from the cover. Even so, *Homunculus*, Womack's third book, operates in a territory close to translation – though one where liberties are taken, such as the use of exclamatory phrases like "jinkies!" and "Let's split up and look for clues!", from the 1960s–'70s animated TV series *Scooby-Doo*.

Womack speaks through Maximian. He also speaks to him initially in a prefatory poem. And Maximian would seem to speak back to Womack; or perhaps he talks only to himself, using the self-appellation "old homunculus". But who is this little man, the generative seedling of the fully formed adult? The author or the persona? An epigraph (written by Womack) – "I, a meta-traveller from an antique land..." – winkingly anticipates the 'meta' nature of the book-length poem to come.

The merging, if it is a merging, between Maximian and Womack, is a strange one because the Maximian of the first section is an old man contemplating his mortality. (Womack is a much younger man.) The poem begins

> I am old.
>
> Oh fuck,
>
> I am old

and continues in a jauntily self-deprecating mode. "Life, what have you got against me, life?" reads like a caricature of an elderly Jewish man with a Yiddish accent shaking his stick at the ceiling. Later, in that same tonal vein, the speaker reveals his personalised number-plate to be "VE15 M1R", a play on the Yiddish phrase "oy vey iz mir" ("woe is me"). At other moments, the speaker slips into French, Spanish and even Russian.

Elsewhere, the voice has a Frederick Seidel tinge. Morbid and crass rhymes interject and sometimes repeat, eg "Roses are red / soon we'll be dead", "By the thumbing of my prick / Something naughty this way skips". A faint echo of Dylan Thomas appears with "Sad old men, aware of their own decay", which could be a line from 'Do Not Go Gentle Into That Good Night'. Yet another phrase sounds very like Larkin: "In the middle of the night, I wake up". None of these are direct quotations; they are gestural. What they gesture to is a male subjectivity that may lack self-awareness. But a possibility for self-awareness in Womack's poem – and also for meta-narrative, which is linked to self-awareness – is expressed in the almost-rhyming lines "To keep two paths with one mind is more than tough, / they say Marx was good at double consciousness". This first section of the book, with its ontological discourse, as the speaker contemplates his decrepitude and mortality, is possibly the strongest. It ends, "My battery is low and it's getting dark."

Sections two, three and four are flashbacks – reminiscences of love affairs, one with a "dark but comely" woman he calls "Liquorice", another with the sharp-tongued "Whiskey", a third with a "white-skinned" woman called "Eider". These shorthand descriptions are uncomfortable – and the gaze is conventional – but the tropes are reversed by the female objects, who have agency, and who freely express their pleasure, disappointment or abjection. In the penultimate section, about an unnamed woman, the object (the woman) becomes the subject: she uses the stage she is given to deliver a "public eulogy to [Maximian's] private parts", a kind of lyric castration. This female speaker adds a third dimension to the Womack-Maximian homunculus, and suggests, in a notably Jungian fashion, a possibility for growth – not only personally but aesthetically. The poet-voice of section one – monolithic, private and male – has evolved into something polyphonic, diachronic and public. *Homunculus*, like *Alisoun Sings*, is an inventive and exhilarating update on the dramatic monologue.

Kathryn Maris's latest collection is The House with Only An Attic and a Basement *(Penguin, 2018).*

EMERGING POWERS

Martha Sprackland, Citadel, *Liverpool University Press, £9.99,* *ISBN 9781789621020*
Romalyn Ante, Antiemetic for Homesickness, *Chatto, £10,* *ISBN 9781784743000*
Will Harris, RENDANG, *Granta, £10.99, ISBN 9781783785599*

Bidisha on history, migration and self-consciousness

. . .

Three strong debuts by much admired young poets bring an array of sharp talent to lockdown-weary readers. *Citadel* by Martha Sprackland comes with an intriguing premise: the poems in the collection were partly inspired by the pretty awful life of the little-remembered sixteenth-century Spanish queen, Juana of Castile, who was the political pawn of her father, husband and son. These history-inspired works shine with a dark brilliance, with Sprackland's rigorous scholarship combined with an artist's eye. Not just Queen Juana, but her courtiers and persecutors alike slink off the page with sly clarity. In 'The Perfect Wife', a renaissance pamphlet on the duties of a good wife instructs that "A woman out of the home [...] is a fish plucked from the water". In 'An Entertainment of Broken Letrillas for Juana at Seventy, Incarcerated at Tordesillas' the register becomes richly Shakespearean as "the angled moth stops / sights to the equinox / and measures off his slow / ruled line over Madrid."

The contemporary poems in *Citadel*, recounting things like visits to an aquarium, eating some roasted peppers, having a toothache and flushing an insect down the loo, seem disappointingly solipsistic, trivial and banal by comparison with the much more interesting and meaningful (if crushingly confined and miserable) life of Queen Juana. A perfect dark allure gleams through each one of Sprackland's history-influenced works. The final poem, 'Transcript', is an extraordinarily vivid dialogue between Juana and the poet, at once grand and intimately chatty: "if you lie so, and I lie like this we can talk like sisters. I am calling you – pick up". I kept feeling throughout reading *Citadel* that – notwithstanding the collection's 2020 Forward Prize shortlisting for best debut collection – there is actually a stunning, mainstream, bestselling historical novelist in here fighting to get out.

Romalyn Ante's *Antiemetic for Homesickness* is an almost unbearably deep and moving poetic love letter: to her mother, an NHS nurse from the Philippines; to memory, language and culture, lost memories and lost stories; and to the entire, invisible workforce of healers, helpers and carers. Ante herself is a nurse and psychotherapist and the supple generosity of her voice and sharply imagined scenes wrung tears from me by the fifth or sixth poem. A heart-wrenching sense of isolation, of people separated from their homelands, and peoples separated from their histories, steeps the pages. In 'A Manananggal Replies to a Child' a storyteller character weighs up the meaning of secrets, histories, superstitions and stories in "a city cremated by its residual light". This lonely urban light suffuses the entire collection, in which scenes are linked by separation and a departing mother must "Bury all the kisses of yesterday in the fold / of your handkerchief" ('Antiemetic for Homesickness'). In 'Invisible Women', Ante's mother walks to work "when the sky is black / and comes out from work when the sky is black", at one point mistaking a dark statue in a square for "a fellow invisible woman".

The collection nimbly avoids clichés about home, identity, race and belonging. Instead, migration is a trade-off, a balance of negative and positive, gains and losses, carefully trodden and movingly depicted in an internationalised world where movement is common: "Let these Duty Free bags distract our loved ones / from the scars on our feet" ('Group Portrait at the Stopover'). Throughout the collection there are sharp snapshots of crisis-points in hospital wards – "I shake the mountains of her shoulders / *If you can hear me, open your eyes*" ('[ ]') – that are painfully relevant to our current times, none more so than when Ante writes, in 'Names', "Listen – can you hear it? The loneliness / of stretchers along A&E corridors".

Ante does not romanticise anything about the past, but she does seek to recapture it, as various characters within the collection debate the value of memory and story. The collection is filtered through with disputed, changed or varying origin stories and questionable superstitions. 'Kayumanggi' recalls a creation myth in which God moulded people from clay but failed on the first few attempts and was only successful "on the third try". Stories and self-mythologising hold little weight in the real world of hard graft and compromise. In 'Eponym', the narrator laments, "I'd like this poem to take you somewhere else / but all I've got is the song of my grandfather / about a fisherman's son." Loss of life, loss of dignity and loss of support haunt the collection, bubbling up with the sheer poignancy of missing someone – as the sequence of poems tagged 'Tape Recordings for Mama' suggests. However, the collection ends on a note of hope and gradual improvement, even settled affection. As the title poem promises, "You will learn to heal the wounds / of their lives and the wounds of yours." If there's any justice in these dark times, *Antiemetic for Homesickness* will become a must-read collection for the present moment.

Will Harris brings his customary dry wit and directness to *RENDANG*. Of the three collections under review, Harris's is the most obviously twenty-first-century in its fresh address, its breezy cosmopolitanism and cast of mobile, international characters – friends referred to casually by name, as if they're friends of the reader too. There isn't a single poem in this collection that isn't cut through with sardonic humour and an absolutely unique, sideways-glancing tone which shakes off all sentimentality but never descends into dismissive cynicism. In 'Mother Country' the narrator, on a long-deferred trip, touches down "into the black / smog of an emerging / power". Instead of the much-romanticised second- or third-generation literary journey to embrace and reconnect with cultural roots, the poem ends with a rueful shrug: "I have no more excuses."

Harris's uniqueness lies in his simultaneous embodiment and puncturing of the 'diaristic poet' identity: many of the works here present scenes that seem to have been directly witnessed or experienced. However, closer reading reveals a cool self-awareness, reflexivity and irony. In 'From the other side of Shooter's Hill', a big block of long lines describes a female character recounting seeing an ambulance passing and then stopping herself – "Don't you dare think about using me / in a poem, making me into some sad female cypher, my life / a series of symbolic events". Then the narrator himself interrupts, defending himself: "If I say this in a poem, it isn't to defer responsibility but because / I reject the possibility of narrating any life other than my own / and need a voice capacious enough to be both me and not-me, / while always clearly being me."

This playful cleverness at once delights and frustrates. *RENDANG* isn't quite the blazer fans of Will Harris (including me) had been waiting for. It works best when Harris has something of substance to recount. Certain motifs repeat throughout, introducing a frisson of unease: there are repeated references to road accidents and deaths, just-seen or just-missed calamities, of tragic lives glimpsed and bypassed. In 'My Name is Dai' the narrator is accosted by a verbiose yet strangely articulate drunk man and remarks, brilliantly, "There are people who relieve themselves / of information like a dog pissing against a streetlamp". In the opening poem, 'Holy Man', the narrator is approached by a hustler in a posh business district near "Restaurants / like high-end clinics, etherized on white wine". Both these poems start off with sharp, prosy observation but ultimately meander and trail off.

The collection works best when Harris comes down off that high sardonic scaffold and leans into the poetic and playful. 'Seven Dreams of Richard Spencer' plays on the idea of dreams and transformation – dreams and their revealing logic are another clear theme in the collection – to riffs on the idea of becoming a cuckold "with the actual gilded horns", then transforming into a cuckoo, then a cucumber and so on. This playfulness opens up creative possibilities which relax Harris's self-consciousness and allow a far more expansive and generous voice out – one that I would love to see more of in his next collection.

Bidisha is a broadcaster, filmmaker and journalist.

NO FIRE RAINED DOWN

Anthony Burgess, Collected Poems, *Carcanet, £25,*
ISBN 9781800170124

Stephen Wilson on a posthumous collected

...

When as a youngish man John Wilson, better known as the novelist Anthony Burgess, submitted a volume of poems to Faber and Faber, T.S. Eliot was kind enough to sweeten the pill of rejection by pointing to three which he said he liked. He told Burgess he regretted that he was not yet ready for publication. Now that he has been dead for nearly thirty years, Carcanet has decided he's ready – for publication of a *Collected Poems*. In fact he's a 'Classic'.

He's a relative youngster in this category, which includes *Gilgamesh*, *Pearl* and Catullus, although being long dead may not be the only criterion for getting in. Modernist innovations in poetic form passed Burgess by (Jonathan Mann, his editor, doesn't agree), but readers can judge for themselves. Granted Burgess likes to play with words and 'intertextualise'; he's mainly fond of narratives, traditional forms and end rhymes. If his poems are transgressive it's their content rather than their linguistic structure that makes them so. Mann places a previously unpublished long polemical rant against censorship, written in iambic rhyming couplets, as an opener. Penned in April 1989, it's a response to the Salman Rushdie affair, which broadens to cover all threats to freedom of speech and artistic expression:

> For long, in Britain, censorship has worked
> In regions where the dark erotic lurked.
> The genitalia, and what they do,
> Or have done to them, were pronounced taboo.

Under cover of wit, Burgess slips in pearls of wisdom: "Here is a slogan sanity must clutch: / 'Belief is dangerous. Don't believe too much.'"

There follows a sequence of selected Petrarchan sonnets translated from the Roman poet Giuseppe Gioachino Belli (1791–1863), titled 'Belli's Blasphemous Bible'. They cover material from both Old and New Testaments. Belli wrote more than 2,000 antipapist diatribes in an ironic, bawdy vernacular, unpublished during his lifetime. He was profoundly conflicted in his attitude to the Church of Rome. On his deathbed he begged his confessor to destroy his poems, but that didn't happen. I like to imagine him now having changed his mind, happy to see them preserved and glad to have found a soulmate in Burgess. The closing sestet of 'Sonnet 30', 'Lot in repose', conveys the flavour:

> Lot's daughters [...] forsook
> Propriety. Here at least was their father.
> They gave him wine with a well-salted pasty.
> When he was drunk they fucked him to a lather,
> Not finding this unnatural or nasty.
> No fire rained down. It seems that God is rather
> Inclined to incest but hates pederasty.

According to Mann, Burgess often wrote on anything to hand, envelopes, matchboxes, scraps of paper etc, and many of the Belli translations are also playfully illustrated, which makes one wish the originals could be seen.

What's odd under this rubric, is that several sonnets not based on biblical sources, not blasphemous and not written by Belli appear. They are Burgess's own bawdy work, seemingly thrown in for good measure. No. 77, 'Two Uses for Ashes' is an example. Based on a couple of sick jokes passed down the paternal Lancashire generations of his family, it tells the story of two women: one kept her husband's ashes and used them as snuff, the other put them in an eggtimer. Their reasons, recounted in Burgess's autobiography, *Little Wilson and Big God* (1986), are funnier told in a Lancashire accent in the non-poetic form.

It's striking just how much of this book focuses on recasting the Bible in irreverent terms. Next poem along is 'Moses', an exercise in versification which Burgess embarked upon as a way of psyching himself up to the job of writing an English script for a six-part Italian television series. He found doing this helpful in establishing a sense of movement and striking the right dialogic note. It's a narrative that takes up more than 200 pages and forms the bulk of this volume. But wait a minute. It turns out not to be a poem at all. In a kind of Magritte moment, Burgess disarms critics with an introductory disclaimer which I'd label *Ceci n'est pas un poème*. In flagrant contradiction to his present editor who writes, "Anthony Burgess was, first and last, a poet", Burgess himself says, "I am not a poet" and "That this work is not poetry there can be no doubt". He wasn't even trying to write poetry. "Moses", he says, "is too far cliché-ridden, simplistic and didactic to be classified as anything other than a piece of sub-literature, pop-craft." Another kind of disclaimer Burgess employed was to attribute his poems to the pen of a fictional character, notably "F.X. Enderby". One cannot help thinking he was coy about owning them himself.

Does it matter what we call them? Poetry, as Burgess points out, resists definition. It evolves over time giving rise to new, sometimes highly infectious variants. In one epoch poems are flowers, in another Japanese knotweed threatening the formal garden. Nonetheless we all distinguish between good and bad. Mann, reluctantly wielding his editorial axe, generally excluded verses that seemed to be "deliberately bad", but even in that category found a few he felt worthy of inclusion. It can be difficult to distinguish them from the simply 'bad', thus 'Pigs Snort from the Yard':

> Pigs snort from the yard
> Above, gulls mew and heckle.
> Memory's shadows speckle
> The blind, with its swinging cord.

Am I missing something?

It would be unfair to characterise it all as doggerel, however there is little in this collection one could describe as arresting, minutely observed, evocative, moving, inspiring, uplifting, or passionate, save for the libretti which are markedly more successful, and Burgess's consuming fascination with the obscene. 'Lullaby', in the section titled 'Words for Music', stands out as a surprisingly tender product of the Burgess pen:

> Out of the desert the wind blows strong, but cool, but cool from
> out of the sea
> The desert burns and the day is long
> But night sends my loved one back to me

But these poems shouldn't be judged for what they are not meant to be. At the level of mildly amusing, sometimes clever, comic and curious verse, they work.

Posthumous collections which boast previously unpublished items and aim at some degree of comprehensiveness are bound to include stuff the author hoarded but didn't take very seriously. Those who have a biographical or scholarly interest in Burgess as a towering twentieth-century literary polymath, will of course find this collection useful. Others who still read the Bible, if there are any, and remain oppressed by an authoritarian religious upbringing, may find it liberating. Needless to say there are those who will find it offensive, but Burgess is now immune to fatwahs.

Jonathan Mann has done a good job pulling the material together. For academics there is an informative introduction, a list of sources and copious endnotes. It's a pity that some poor copy-editing has marred them. It looks as if there should have been a note attached to 'Sonnet 77', mentioned previously, but instead there are ten lines that belong to 'Sonnet 78', which are then repeated.

In promoting his subject as an important poet, Mann reminds us that his work has been read and enjoyed by millions of people and his verse performed on screens all over the world. Perhaps, but it's difficult to see this book achieving that degree of popularity. Burgess's novels will continue to be read, the product of what he called the writer's struggle to control that intractable enemy – language. I'd say he's left us a legacy of poetic prose and prosaic poems.

Stephen Wilson is an old man whose mother was inclined to burst into 'Kubla Khan' given the slightest opportunity. He has had a lifelong interest in poetry.

FOCUSED BREVITY

Anna Selby, Field Notes, *Hazel Press, £10, ISBN 9781838081607*
Ella Duffy, Rootstalk, *Hazel Press, £10, ISBN 9781838081621*
Matthew Hollis, Leaves, *Hazel Press, £10, ISBN 9781838081614*
Simone Atangana Bekono, how the first sparks became visible, *tr. David Colmer, The Emma Press, £6.50, ISBN 9781912915552*
Katherine Lockton, Paper Doll, *Flipped Eye, £4, ISBN 9781905233601*
Jo Young, Firing Pins, *Ink, Sweat & Tears/Café Writers, £7.50, ISBN 9780992725334*
Gail McConnell, Fothermather, *Ink, Sweat & Tears/Café Writers, £7.50, ISBN 9780992725341*
John Glenday, The Firth, *Mariscat, £6, ISBN 9781916060968*

Dzifa Benson on the unique propositions of eight pamphlets

. . .

Pamphlets are often thought of as nothing more than a new poet's calling card, yet the focused brevity of a good pamphlet can distil a poet's concerns so precisely that it can be more deeply affecting than a full-length collection. Consider the award-winning Warsan Shire, whose reputation as an uncommon poet of belonging and displacement has been built on the strength of just three coruscating pamphlets (collaborations with Beyoncé notwithstanding), belying the notion that the full-length collection is king. It's gratifying to see that many more established as well as emerging poets are beginning to take advantage of the format's unique proposition, with these eight pamphlets as evidence.

Pamphlets don't come more covetable and elegant in design than a trio from the freshly minted Hazel Press, specialising in ecological poetry. Anna Selby's *Field Notes* reports from the extremes of ecological enquiry with several poems written in waterproof notebooks while studying marine life underwater in the Atlantic Ocean. These poems shimmer and undulate, pulsing with a languorous earthiness that plugs directly into the pamphlet's epigraph, by Joan Didion: "what it is like to be a woman, the irreconcilable difference of it – that sense of living one's deepest life underwater, that dark involvement with blood and birth and death".

These intimate poems of transformation delight with their attention to the nuances of meaning and sound, tracking the persistence of life even in the most inhospitable of places. They brim with sensual imagery that collapses hierarchical boundaries between humankind and the rest of nature. Many of the poems, especially the ones in the section titled 'Notes from the Water', made me wonder about the juncture between the scientific rigour of gathering empirical data and the licence that is necessary to tip it into the realm of poetry. It's not surprising to read that these specific poems were transcribed verbatim. While they have some poetic traction, their list-like form prevents them from shifting into the transcendence that characterises the rest of the book. This is far from the case for the standout poem of the collection, the astonishingly effective 'What Happens to a Heart'.

If Selby approaches ecological concerns from a place of love, in contrast her label-mate and former Foyle Young Poet of the Year Ella Duffy has said that her poems explore the sinister side of nature. *Rootstalk* is a spare, phantasmagoric long poem that tracks Epipogium aphyllum, the ghost orchid, what the poet calls a "decade-wintered flower". This recently discovered rare orchid spends most of its life underground and flowers just once every ten years, briefly surfacing then retreating back into the darkness of the earth. Places where the plant grows are kept secret, adding to its magical allure which, in turn, informs the dreamlike world of the pamphlet.

Voiced by a chorus of five women reimagined from history and mythology – mother and daughter Demeter and Persephone, lovers Mae and Esther, and a young girl, Cora, the pamphlet has a dramatic quality that I can imagine being performed as theatre. This dramatic tilt is a canny device. It enables the different voice registers to quickly and smoothly shimmer in and out of focus, somewhat like an impressionist painting. This fragmentary, otherworldly effect perfectly suits the overarching conceit of the poem in which all the characters search for literal and metaphorical items – patience, water, redemption, mushrooms, a song, the orchid itself – while Demeter is, of course, searching for Persephone in the underworld domain of the orchid. Duffy might be a relatively new poet but she writes with the kind of verve and intelligence that heralds an exciting poetic future.

Seven years in the making, Matthew Hollis's long poem *Leaves* explores loss and catharsis in the form of a conversation between a father and daughter during a walk through autumn woods. Loosely based on Eastern ideas of the elements wood, fire, earth, metal and water, it isn't too fanciful to call this poem a song of seasonal degeneration and rejuvenation on account of its use of subtle musical effects; the poet is highly attuned to the nuance of sound. It isn't surprising then to learn that Hollis is also a guitarist who is interested in the confluence between poetry and music. The poem's songlike quality lends it an incantatory rhythm that quietly but insistently interrogates the ecological future of the planet and laments the carelessness with which it is treated. Obviously, the daughter represents future generations here and, appropriately, makes the kind of declarations and asks the stumping questions that children are wont to do of older "worn mind[s]", which leads the speaker to question his notion of time:

> Soon you will tell me you can touch your own shadow,
> that you're angry at the sea because the waves won't listen;
> you'll wonder why the moon doesn't bump into the earth,
> and say you see gravity falling.
> Daddy, it's boiling dark out there. I will
> always be here for you if you don't need me.

The grief embedded in that last couplet is a theme worn lightly throughout, even as the overarching tone tends towards hope. This is the kind of poem that makes a reader wish Hollis could be a little more prolific.

Poet and novelist Simone Atangana Bekono's award-winning debut pamphlet, *how the first sparks became visible*, translated here by David Colmer, was first published in the Netherlands as *hoe de eerste vonken zichtbaar waren*. It largely eschews punctuation, which lends Bekono's epistolary exploration of race, gender and sexuality a dislocating, confessional, stream-of-consciousness that recalls Bhanu Kapil's T.S. Eliot

Prize-winning *How To Wash a Heart*. It suits these very direct poems that trouble the intersection between corporeality and identity and are somewhat reminiscent of the aforementioned Warsan Shire's poetic diction. This notion of intersectionality is never more problematic than in the poet's acute awareness of having a black female body while living in a country like the Netherlands in which the speaker of the poems declares "I am the white Western male's thought experiment". It's difficult to assert an identity when systemic oppression in society erases your existence to the near invisibility of a silhouette:

> I was born in a forest
>
> I was born and someone trained a light on me
> on the birthing cloth behind me, my silhouette appeared
>
> My silhouette opened her mouth and said
> 'I exist because your body exists
> Cronos devouring his children
> as bloodthirsty as Goya painted him
> a body become unrecognisable
> greedy and chaotic
> not rooted in the earth'
> this was all I had to go on

Bekono writes with a ferocious verve and visceral urgency, the realm of the body sprawling in long lines as the poetry pours onto the page. I can't wait to see where she turns next.

Occupying similar but less satisfyingly wild terrain in their interrogation of identity in crises, the poems of Anglo-Bolivian poet Katherine Lockton in *Paper Doll* are much more distilled in their form and content – a kind of lean-meat-on-bones poetry – than Bekono's rangy lines. The way these poems sit so neatly on the page belies the seismic, emotional commotion they attempt to corral into see-through language. Lockton's survival of a fall from a building aged four and, later, a traumatising sexual assault give this collection its narrative traction. The poems don't always succeed in their intention. Perhaps this is precisely because the chaotic, messy experiences behind it – failure, grief, loss, unrequited love, sexual assault – mean the poems require a more untrammelled approach in execution on the page.

The urge to rigidly control one's environment, even one's poetry-making environment, following trauma is understandable. One considers the fragility inherent in the book's title and the reaction of the mother in the sequence poem 'The Rape Scene': "Your mother says it isn't rape / because he is younger than you. Did you rape him?" But tightly controlled emotions do not make for affecting poetry. In combination with unnecessarily repeating the same tropes across several poems, an on-the-nose-diction and frequent over-explication in the last lines of poems, it's a shame that this "landmark for the UK's Latinx community" isn't more sure of itself.

A duo of pamphlets from the winners of the Ink Sweat & Tears/Café Writers Pamphlet Commission Competition – Jo Young's *Firing Pins* and Gail McConnell's *Fothermather* – push into the seldom charted poetic territories of servicewomen and queer parenthood. When we think of war poetry we still tend to default to the work of First World War poets such as Wilfred Owen and Siegfried Sassoon on frontline combat, but more recently, poetry collections like Kevin Powers' *Letter Composed During a Lull in the Fighting* (2014) have foregrounded the dislocation of struggling to slot back into civilian society in the aftermath of combat. Even so, most war poetry is told from the point of view of men, and Young's poetry in *Firing Pins* subverts stereotypical gender roles and military language to remind the reader that women have been far from passive observers of conflict. As such, while I read the pamphlet, I was aware of an underlying question: what can this also say about our conceptions of masculinity?

This pamphlet is emphatically situated in the realm of womanhood, reflecting the collision of duties, wants and natural inclinations. Young, who has served in the British Army for over two decades and has seen active, sometimes frightening, duty in Afghanistan, highlights this in the introduction: "The soldier is someone who falls in and out of love, gives birth, battles her body, argues with old school friends, falls ill and gets well again, finds a joy in soldiering and matches it with despair of battlefields, feels homesick and has very mixed views about authority figures and geo-politics. Nevertheless, she soldiers." Appropriating the language of sighting through a rifle in response to army regulations on cosmetics, Young leans right into the conflict inherent in wanting to be seen in the multivalency of her femininity in the first poem, 'L'Oréal Paris Infallible Gel Crayon Eyeliner in Browny Crush':

I want those layers leaden,
galenic, Coptic magic full of ritual
and embalming kajal – I want to beam
all their through rifle sights.
I want it helmet-hidden.

As much as it reveals about a female soldier's mentality, the pamphlet is also complicated by what it doesn't address or what I suspect Young is careful to avoid – culpability, victimhood and a philosophy about the necessity of war. It would be fascinating to see how Young might address these by drawing from a richer, bolder canvas in a full-length collection.

To say that McConnell's *Fothermather* is about queer parenthood is to over-simplify its intentions and execution. The neologism – "a nonsense word that tells the truth" – of the title alerts the reader to the fact that this pamphlet is also an exercise in subverting what the poet calls "audible linguistic colonization" through the struggle to forge her identity regarding her son, "Finn, the brilliantist", of whom she is a non-biological parent. Through a series of epiphanies resulting from Finn's gestation and birth rendered into concretism via the metaphor of a seahorse, what started out as a comparatively straightforward ambition to interrogate gender-non-conforming parenthood, is refracted into a more layered and often gnomic contemplation of how things come to be named, how language cleaves into meaning, "how forms are improvised and adapted in creaturely communication".

That overarching seahorse imagery isn't quite as outlandish as it might first seem. It's a relatively easy leap of the imagination to see how an ultrasound image of a foetus could resemble a seahorse, but a seahorse is also emblematic of non-conforming parenting – it's the male seahorse who gestates the eggs. A seahorse's morphology, according to the poet, is made up of the "head of a horse", "belly of a kangaroo" and the "tail of a monkey" – the identity of a parent can be several things, fluid, not fixed:

I am neither   the female Seahorse who lays the eggs,
    nor   the male Seahorse who carries them.

I am   not quite either and a little of both.

Those spaces between words, an example of the concretism and erasure that distinguishes this pamphlet, perform the disorientation and struggle of redefining identity on the page. They are wielded with skill to blow open convention in the title poem, an innovative villanelle that unpacks the neologism. With the news that Penned in the Margins has acquired McConnell's full-length debut collection, there is plenty more to hear from McConnell in the not too distant future.

In interview, John Glenday has called the poems in *The Firth*, his first publication since *The Golden Mean* (2015), "worked memories". What does this mean exactly? An attempt to hazard a guess leads to the words 'working memory', loosely defined as the information someone must remember long enough to use it. That definition certainly holds poetic appeal but doesn't seem to pin down Glenday's notion precisely. While not understanding the term doesn't interfere with a reader's enjoyment of the compressed lyricism of these spare, tautly intimate poems, one suspects that knowing what the poet means would facilitate a deeper reading. In the absence of further elucidation, I define "worked memories" as the process of capturing something as nebulous and abstract as a memory and attaching it, via language, to something in the material world. This is what happens in the sequence poem 'nine coastal birds' and five separate poems called 'wild flower', which seem to root the characteristics of Scottish people in their country's wild flowers, such as the thistle.

Another sequence poem, 'metamorphoses', takes that movement from intangibility to tangibility and layers it with Greek mythology, itself a concept that borders on abstraction, but in Glenday's skilled hands demonstrates why mythology is a useful tool for making sense of twenty-first-century concerns which are themselves also eternal. An example of this is the first section of the sequence in which the speaker compares his mother to Leda. It is often repeated that Glenday excels at writing from quietly observed places and this pamphlet makes it evident why. This isn't bells and whistles poetry but it is nevertheless deeply affecting in its muted but precisely controlled assurance.

Dzifa Benson is a poet and dramatist who writes about poetry for various publications.

THE NATIONAL POETRY COMPETITION 2020

Judges: Neil Astley, Jonathan Edwards and Karen McCarthy Woolf

The judges share comments below on the top three winners in the National Poetry Competition 2020 – Marvin Thompson, Iain Twiddy and Jack Nicholls. These poems are published for the first time here. All ten winning poems can be read in the National Poetry Competition anthology and on The Poetry Society website.

First prize: Marvin Thompson, 'The Fruit of the Spirit is Love (Galatians 5:22)'
Marvin Thompson's poem operates on multiple, complex levels yet speaks in a voice that is fresh, honest and brave. Specific in its geography, natural in diction, the poem asks many distinctly contemporary questions: what is it to raise dual-heritage children in the UK, and specifically in Wales? How does black identity shape itself in a white environment, where allegiance to a predominantly hostile flag is the paradox of belonging? Will these children be loyal to Wu-Tang or sing hymns in the Welsh choir? Or, as the poem demonstrates, will they do all of these things at once, in a manner that is seemingly effortless? These are big questions, which, one might argue, only the best poetry is fit to answer. That Thompson does so with such concision and formal dexterity is a delight – the villanelle being the perfect choice for such enduring existential enquiry. In addition the poem's biblical intertextuality provides a historical and spiritual context that situates it as a work in conversation with the Caribbean and diaspora. That it includes the word *cwtch* can only be a bonus.

Second prize: Iain Twiddy, 'Fence'
This is a beautiful poem about the relationship between children and parents, the sense we stumble on in adulthood that our parents, these gods we've known all our lives, are human beings, who had a life before we showed up. There's a wonderful description of the connection between mothers and children – "this person I lived in, who grew me" – and we judges really enjoyed

the way the poem goes to town on the spoken sound of the word "mum", "a *hmm* like a fish glumly swallowing". The thing that allows this poem to achieve absolute greatness is its long final sentence. Strung so masterfully across multiple line and stanza breaks, the considerable technical achievement here contributes to the more important thing about this sentence – its great emotional impact. The overall effect here is of a deeply moving empathetic connection between the speaker and the mother's imagined experience.

Third prize: Jack Nicholls, 'Mum with Sword'

In 'Mum with Sword' a child's transforming imagination becomes at the same time the poet's power to turn things into metaphors. The speaker of this obsessively playful, multi-layered poem turns what may be the mother's plastic yellow birdseed scoop into what may be a four-foot long "bastard sword" inexplicably held by the mother as she walks about the garden and the house. It exists as a sword in the poem for as long as the childlike speaker and the poet tells us it is a sword, but the poet knows that "you may terminate my contract / if you choose", through disbelief, whereupon this poem will cease to exist as a poem. We loved the way this poem plays with its own reality as well as with the reader's perception. The speaker could be someone suffering from hallucinations in which what we see is transformed into something else, metamorphosed, as in the act of writing the poem. Is the speaker remembering a childhood game with the mother holding a pretend sword, or is this a phantom sword perceived by someone whose grip on reality is somewhat unstable?

...

National Poetry Competition 2020 Winners

First Prize: Marvin Thompson,
'The Fruit of the Spirit is Love (Galatians 5:22)'
Second Prize: Iain Twiddy, 'Fence'
Third Prize: Jack Nicholls, 'Mum with Sword'

Commended:
Luke Allan, 'Something to Show for It' • Marie Baléo, 'Peregrines'
Daniel Bennett, 'Clickbait' • Susannah Hart, 'Song of my auntie'
Jennifer Hyde, 'Lifesaving' • Vanessa Lampert, 'Sand'
Mark Pajak, 'Trick'

MARVIN THOMPSON

The Fruit of the Spirit is Love (Galatians 5:22)

Dusk reddened a Dual Heritage neck, hands
and a moustache – its ends curled with wax. Jason Lee?
I stood below his dreadlocks in woodland

and reached up to touch his feet. A whirring fan
greeted my waking eyes, the house sleepy.
I'd dreamt both Dali's Christ and someone hanged.

"... a pineapple on his head..." sang football fans
and a comedian blacked up as Jason Lee,
mocking Rastas. Did Jason beg Jah:

"Please keep this from my kids." Should I tell mine
I filled my lungs with '90s minstrelsy
and sang, a teen lost in lads' mag England?

Who taught me pro-Black talk was contraband?
The me who cwtched Dad whilst watching Spike Lees
was shoved down basement stairs, feet tied to hands.

Embarrassed, should I play my kids Wu-Tang
and other rap that set my rebel free?
One day, when they walk their kids through woodland
will they sing calypsos or 'Blood of the Lamb'?

IAIN TWIDDY

Fence

Landline, long-distance, he tells me about the fall:
her coming home through the field by the river, alone,
trying to climb over the sheep fence;

then the earthy fact, the impact of lying there
in the damp grass, the edge-of-winter mud
where the sheep step, where the dogs sniff and lift,

trying to drag up, broken-hipped, waiting for a passerby not to,
when this slips out, like a hushed admission:
She's always had quite poor balance, he says –

and it hits me, like thin ice on the lake,
not the way she could never ride a bike
like the other mums, never put her head

underwater, never let us go *all that way*
to try ice-skating in Peterborough;
but the fact that he doesn't say *mum*.

It's like a glimpse of soft skin under armour,
the pink of the tongue behind the mostly closed lips.
Not *mum*, that almost-mumble, like a stone

gulped by water, that self-censoring numb,
a *hmm* like a fish glumly swallowing,
that repetitive sense that whatever she said

was without question / welcomely accepted.
She, he says, an open sustain, a free
unsmothered, unhooded from motherhood,

the *shh* whispering into the secret
that this person I lived in, who grew me,
has existed for him longer than me,

in a way he alone in the world knows.
It's as if I can hear for the first time
from under the constructions of marriage

and parenthood, from under the rubble
of the collapses of body and brain,
that *She* like the most belling appeal,

the simplest underpinning principle;
as if I've been given a close-in glimpse
of them in the beginning, stepping out

in a sheep field near Corbridge, would it be,
the river grinding out of the winter,
him helping her over a fence, maybe,

her heart not skipping a beat, but leaping.

JACK NICHOLLS

Mum with Sword

My mum carries a sword now. You misunderstand me. My mum
carries a sword now. My mum has a long, solemn sword

swinging behind her when she turns to put the birdseed
in the feeder. It is very strange seeing my mum on the settee

holding her four-foot bastard sword. I don't want to talk
about the pheasants stalking round the garden singing for grapes.

I am still getting used to my mum's new sword. If I am truthful,
I am not ready to be addressing my mum's sword

in a poem. Currently, I am not fit for work, and though I can self-certify
for a few poems, soon I will have to have a proper, proper chat with myself.

You might wonder what my mum's new sword looks like,
or if there is medieval detailing on the scabbard

that a healthy poem would illuminate. Picturing my mum as a
lovely woman with cool specs and smart dyed hair,

as she is, you might wonder how she bears the weight of the thing.
Is she struggling? Are veins cording her biceps? Will her cardie snag

and balled tissues come tumbling from the sleeve? You might wonder why,
when I'm wholly aware that I must satisfy you of my health, my capacity

to perform my duties, when I know that you may terminate my contract
if you choose, why I have doodled a sword on a soggy, salty napkin.

Friends, I couldn't stop shouting in the garden.
This isn't easy for you either. Stick to the rules:

you're allowed to now pronounce me *arsehole* out of earshot
and I'm allowed to trail long smears of cold cream on the castle walls,

and blink like an alien into a tall Gothic mirror, and feel as empty
as a plastic yellow birdseed scoop. My mum poured it

into my hand and the pheasants came running, and, though wild
and wanting other things, they ate, just like she said they would,

they fed from the flat of my hand. My mum's sword was drawn, crudely,
and lay amongst the daisies. It looked solemn. It looked long.

It looked like a sword. I looked at it and I wrote *sword*.
Friends, take me tightly in both hands and swing.

CONTRIBUTORS

Jason Allen-Paisant is a Jamaican poet whose first collection will be published in 2021 by Carcanet • **Paula Bohince** is the author of three collections, most recently *Swallows and Waves* • **Marianne Boruch**'s tenth poetry collection is *The Anti-Grief* (Copper Canyon, 2019). Her prose includes three essay collections and a memoir, *The Glimpse Traveler* (Indiana, 2011) • **Beverley Bie Brahic**'s latest collections are *The Hotel Eden* (Carcanet) and *Baudelaire: Invitation to the Voyage* (Seagull) • **Kit Buchan** is a conservation journalist living in the Midlands. His musical, *The Season*, co-written with Jim Barne, won the Stiles & Drewe and Stage Debut awards for new musical theatre • **Mary Jean Chan** is the author of *Flèche* (Faber, 2019). She is Senior Lecturer in Creative Writing at Oxford Brookes • **Geraldine Clarkson**'s fourth pamphlet, *Crucifox*, is forthcoming from Verve in May • **Angela Cleland** is a poet and novelist. Her most recent collection is *Room of Thieves* (Salt, 2013) • **Natalie Crick** is a research student at Newcastle University • **Tarik Dobbs** is an Arab American, queer writer born in Dearborn, Michigan • **Samatar Elmi**'s debut pamphlet *Portrait of Colossus* is published by Flipped Eye • **Helen Farish**'s most recent collections are *The Dog of Memory* and *Nocturnes at Nohant* • **Amlanjyoti Goswami**'s debut collection is *River Wedding* (Poetrywala, 2019) • **John Greening**'s most recent books are *The Silence* (Carcanet) and *Vapour Trails: Reviews and Essays on Poetry* (Shoestring) • **Vona Groarke**'s latest poetry collection is *Double Negative* (Gallery, 2019) • **Hagiwara Sakutarō** (1886–1942) was a Japanese poet, aphorist, and literary and cultural critic active during the Taishō and Shōwa periods and a forerunner of modernist poetry in Japan • **Ishion Hutchinson** is the author of *Far District* and *House of Lords and Commons*. He directs the graduate writing programme at Cornell University • **Jae Kim** is a fiction writer and a literary translator. He is currently pursuing a PhD in comparative literature at Princeton • **Dominic Leonard** received an Eric Gregory Award in 2019. His pamphlet, *Antimasque*, will be published by Broken Sleep this year • **Tarn MacArthur** is a PhD candidate at the University of St Andrews and is at work on his first collection of poems • **Richie McCaffery** is the author of two collections from Nine Arches. His most recent publication is a pamphlet, *First Hare* (Mariscat, 2020) • **Gail McConnell**'s *Fothermather* was shortlisted for the Michael Marks Award. *The Sun is Open* will be published by Penned in the Margins in September • **Jamie McKendrick**'s latest publications are *Anomaly* (2018), a poetry collection; *The Years* (2020), an illustrated chapbook; and a book of essays, *The Foreign Connection* (2020) • **Valzhyna Mort**'s third book of poetry *Music for the Dead and Resurrected* came out in 2020 from FSG • **Mohammad S. Razai** was born in Kabul in 1986 and came to Britain at fifteen. He works as a doctor in the NHS • **Hannah Regel** is the author of *Oliver Reed* (Montez, 2020). She lives in London • **Will Stone** is a poet, essayist and literary translator from French and German. His most recent poetry collection was *The Slowing Ride* (Shearsman, 2020) • **Stephanie Sy-Quia**'s debut poetic work, *Amnion*, is forthcoming from Granta in November • **Erkut Tokman** is a Turkish poet, editor, translator and interviewer. He has published five collections of poetry.

Image by Kate Dehler. katedehler.com

L to r: Gail McConnell, Jamie McKendrick (photo: Caroline Forbes) and Stephanie Sy-Quia

The Poetry Society Annual Lecture Series 2021

In association with University of Liverpool

Terrance Hayes

Wednesday 28 April
7pm BST, via ZOOM

Book online at bit.ly/annuallecturethayes

Tickets are FREE but must be reserved.
Donations welcome

m nourbeSe philip

Wednesday 3 November
7pm GMT, via ZOOM

Book online at bit.ly/annuallecturephilip

Tickets are FREE but must be reserved.
Donations welcome

The Poetry Society and University of Liverpool's Centre for New and International Writing have teamed up to present three online lectures in 2021, and are delighted to announce that the acclaimed poets **Terrance Hayes** and **m nourbeSe philip** will give lectures as part of the series.

Each lecture will feature a live Q & A and the poets will read a selection of their poems, chosen to respond to their themes.

The Poetry Society Annual Lecture Series 2021 is presented by The Poetry Society in association with University of Liverpool (as the Kenneth Allott lectures). The first lecture in the series was given by Valzhyna Mort on 2 March 2021. All three lectures will be published in *The Poetry Review*.

THEPOETRYSOCIETY

UNIVERSITY OF LIVERPOOL Centre for New and International Writing

Supported using public funding by ARTS COUNCIL ENGLAND